Instructor's Manual to Accompany

Voices and Values:
A Reader for Writers

Janet M. Goldstein

Beth Johnson

TOWNSEND PRESS

Books in the Townsend Press Reading Series:

Groundwork for College Reading
Ten Steps to Building College Reading Skills
Ten Steps to Improving College Reading Skills
Ten Steps to Advancing College Reading Skills

Books in the Townsend Press Vocabulary Series:

Vocabulary Basics
Groundwork for a Better Vocabulary
Building Vocabulary Skills
Building Vocabulary Skills, Short Version
Improving Vocabulary Skills
Improving Vocabulary Skills, Short Version
Advancing Vocabulary Skills
Advancing Vocabulary Skills, Short Version
Advanced Word Power

Other Reading and Writing Books:

Everyday Heroes
English at Hand
A Basic Reader for College Writers
The Townsend Thematic Reader

Send book orders and requests for desk copies or supplements to:
Townsend Press Book Center
1038 Industrial Drive
West Berlin, New Jersey 08091

For even faster service, contact us in any of the following ways:
By telephone: 1-800-772-6410
By fax: 1-800-225-8894
By e-mail: townsendcs@aol.com
Through our website: www.townsendpress.com

Instructor's Manual to Accompany *Voices and Values: A Reader for Writers*
Copyright © 2002 by Townsend Press
ISBN 0-944210-11-2

Contents

Guided Writing Assignments   49

To the Instructor

In this supplement to *Voices and Values: A Reader for Writers*, we offer some suggestions intended to help you use the book with students. While many instructors develop their own techniques for using a textbook, these suggestions will provide you with a starting point. Based on our experience in the classroom, we believe these ideas will help you create an environment where lively discussion occurs as students genuinely engage with the ideas, concepts, questions, and challenges raised by the readings. Within the setting of those discussions, students can begin to formulate and refine the ideas that will eventually serve as the bases for the paragraphs and essays they will produce.

Voices and Values is based on two premises: (1) that reading and writing are interrelated activities, and (2) that students learn best through doing: they learn to be better readers and writers by reading and writing. The inherent problem for many students, of course, is finding material that they *want* to read, and coming up with topics that they *want* to write about. To that end, we have chosen forty readings that examine and celebrate universal human values—values whose consequences we encounter at every stage of our lives. For instance, the readings raise questions such as "Why do some students bully others?" "Does television literally make us stupid?" "What do children owe their parents?" and "How should we deal with angry feelings?" Students will find people, situations, and controversies in these forty readings that will interest them and stimulate their thinking. In addition to the readings, *Voices and Values* provides a generous number of writing assignments, encouraging students to explore, within the context of their own lives, ideas raised in the readings.

GETTING STARTED

While you may decide not to proceed through the book from beginning to end, preferring to assign readings on the basis of student interests or your own instructional goals, we recommend that you introduce your students to *Voices and Values* by assigning its two brief opening chapters, "Becoming a Better Reader" and "Becoming a Better Writer." Both chapters emphasize the concept of point and support. Throughout *Voices and Values*, students are consistently reminded that making a point and supporting that point is the cornerstone of effective reading and writing.

"Becoming a Better Reader"

In "Becoming a Better Reader," fill-in-the-blank questions help students familiarize themselves with the format of the forty reading selections. Five reading strategies are then introduced. These strategies are reinforced in the questions that follow each selection. Those questions require students to (1) understand vocabulary in context, (2) recognize the central point and main ideas presented in the reading, (3) identify key supporting details, (4) draw inferences, and (5) be aware of the writer's craft (including types of introduction and conclusion, types of support, patterns of organization, tone, purpose, audience, and titles). Depending upon the emphasis of your course, you may wish to return to this introductory chapter in the weeks to come in order to, for example, give more in-depth attention to a particular reading strategy.

"Becoming a Better Writer"

In "Becoming a Better Writer," we provide students with helpful tips on writing a paragraph and, in greater depth, writing an essay. In addition to making a point and supporting that point, we present a third goal in writing: organizing the supporting material. Students are thus shown the entire writing process—from techniques of prewriting and preparing a scratch outline through writing the first and subsequent drafts through editing the final paper. Depending upon the emphasis of your course, you may wish to return to this chapter in the weeks to come in order to, for example, give more in-depth attention to a particular step in the writing process.

(Note that if you are teaching a writing course, you can easily use *Voices and Values* as a supplemental anthology. The high-interest essays are engagingly written, and you will find the exercises helpful in focusing students' attention on the fundamentals of effective writing. If you choose to organize your course thematically, you will find such suggested groupings in the first Table of Contents. An Alternate Table of Contents is provided for instructors who prefer to organize their courses according to traditional rhetorical modes.)

Writing Assignments in the Book

The activities that accompany the reading selections offer a great many opportunities for writing of all kinds. First of all, the four writing assignments (two paragraphs, two essays) that follow each reading use the selection as a springboard, but go on to provide a wide variety of topics from which students may choose. The assignments also offer the student writer various types and degrees of assistance. Some topics suggest thesis statements, supporting points, and organizational patterns, while others require students to supply their own material. Some assignments invite students to write about personal concerns; others require students to state and support their own observations about larger issues. Secondly, the "First Impressions" topics that precede each selection and the discussion questions that follow each selection can be used as additional writing assignments, should you need them. Finally, there are twenty "Additional Writing Assignments" beginning on page 461 of the textbook. These assignments require students to read two essays from the book, then write a paper that brings together a theme central to both selections with their own experience or observations. These challenging assignments encourage students to think more deeply, recognizing that the human value being focused upon is something that exists far outside the confines of a single reading selection.

(Note that when the additional writing assignments are added to the "First Impressions" topics, the discussion questions, and the paragraph and essay assignments for the forty readings, *Voices and Values* gives students **460** possibilities for writing!)

For students who need more guidance in how to proceed, this manual includes ten guided writing assignments (pages 49–75), five paragraph assignments and five essay assignments, that show the step-by-step process a student might use in writing a paper on this topic. You may wish to photocopy one or more of these guided assignments and use them as the basis for individual or classroom instruction.

VARYING THE APPROACH

Working on *Voices and Values* as a class will be a different experience for every teacher. What finally happens will, of course, depend on the class dynamic, your particular teaching style, the purpose of each class meeting, and the familiarity of the students with the material. In our experience, varying our instructional methods—using a combination of whole-class discussion, small-group collaborative learning, conferencing with the teacher, and individualized instruction—helps ensure success for the greatest number of students possible and, quite simply, makes class more interesting for everyone.

Whole-Class Discussion

As you introduce *Voices and Values* to your students, we suggest that you spend time familiarizing students with the book's format. Assigning students the first two chapters— "Becoming a Better Reader" and "Becoming a Better Writer"— and requiring them to complete the exercises included there will assist them in this regard.

But consider spending time in classroom discussion about reading and writing in general. Talk together, for example, about the five "Reading Strategies" (pages 4–9 in the book), the construction of a paragraph or a formal essay (pages 12–20), and the book's emphasis on *point and support*. These sessions can lay the groundwork for the more detailed examination of specific reading selections and the associated writing activities to follow.

It is also valuable, at this stage of the class, to work as a class through a reading selection and its accompanying exercises. For this session, we recommend using the first essay, "Bird Girl," beginning on page 31 of the text. Each of the activities for this selection is explained fully, and answers are provided, along with explanations of these answers, so that students will know exactly what to do when they turn to the other readings in the book. Discuss the varying expectations students have after reading the selection's Preview. Point out that each Word to Watch is, for easy reference, accompanied by the number of the paragraph in which it first occurs. Then, as a class, read the selection aloud. Give students a few minutes to jot down some answers to the questions appearing in First Impressions, and then ask them to share their responses. Their varying answers will stimulate discussion and can lead students to consider perspectives other than their own. Similarly, working through the Vocabulary Check and Reading Check together will give students immediate feedback if they have marked incorrect responses, and you can help clarify why one answer is better than the others.

The Discussion Questions that follow each reading can stimulate valuable exploration of ideas and debate. One technique we like to use in class is this: After hearing a student's answer to a particular question, we ask to hear from someone who strongly disagrees with him or her. Next we call on someone who disagrees with the second speaker. In each case, of course, we ask that the speaker explain the reasons for his or her opinion. Another technique we like involves using a continuum, or range of responses—especially if the discussion question asks students if they think something was right or wrong, justified or unjustified, etc. For example, after the Jackie Robinson story "He Was First," we ask if Robinson's manager was right to ask Robinson not to fight back against the people who threw racial taunts at him. In such a case, we like to put a horizontal line on the board, with "Strongly agree" at one end and "Strongly disagree" at the other. We then ask students to go to the board and arrange themselves at the point on the line that best represents their opinion. The discussion that ensues often helps clarify students' own thinking as well as open their minds to others' perspectives.

If the classroom conversation is slow in starting, you can refer to the Suggested Answers (beginning on page 19 of this manual) and get the ball rolling with your own input. Note that these suggested answers are not exhaustive; students often come up with surprising and original responses that reflect their personal interpretations and private experiences. These suggested answers, then, are merely guides to discussion, particularly useful if students are hesitant in how to begin to approach or answer a question, or if students need to be refocused on the selection should their responses veer too far off track. Sometimes further questions are provided to lead students to think more deeply or more broadly about a topic or a controversial issue. The best responses, of course, often occur spontaneously, in the dynamics of student interaction. When that kind of magic happens, teachers would do well to close this *Instructor's Manual* and simply become participants in the discussion.

Collaborative Work

For many students, working in groups of two to four offers the most favorable environment for discussion and learning. While there are advantages to hearing input from a large number of classmates, many students are reluctant to speak out in a whole-class discussion. Instructors may find it difficult to draw less outgoing students into a discussion dominated by those eager to speak. Also, students who are less prepared for class find it relatively easy to escape notice in a whole-classroom discussion. In a small collaborative group, students are called upon to participate in the creation and revision of ideas. The environment stimulates active learning, rather than passive reception of information.

Collaborative work can be accomplished in a variety of ways. One simple approach is to group students and then have them answer the Reading Check questions for a particular selection. Together, the students will decide which response best completes each item. If there is disagreement, students will have to go back to the primary authority, the selection itself, to find evidence that seems reasonable to the entire group. Students not only enjoy the debate and brief investigation that shows the rest of the class that they are right, but they also learn in a natural and practical setting the value of textual evidence and the importance of checking and testing their ideas before presenting them as fact.

An essential key to making group work successful is to provide students with clear guidelines for doing what they are expected to do. Although the instructions for the exercises are clearly stated, students' self-consciousness in a group setting can cause them to "freeze," unsure of how to express themselves or respond to others' comments. A useful (and enjoyable) way to model the group process is to ask three or four volunteers to meet with you outside of class to rehearse a role-playing activity. In class, then, your volunteer group can dramatize first *ineffective* and then *effective* group responses. Laughing together over the unhelpful nature of ineffective responses (plan to allow for some humorous exaggeration!) will set the stage for students to work together in a relaxed and constructive manner.

Sharing one another's paragraphs and essays in small groups can be an extremely effective instructional tool. For example, many beginning writers cannot tell when their own work is unclear. To hear "I don't understand what you mean here" from their peers can be as valuable as hearing the same comment from an instructor. Bear in mind, though, the importance of providing clear guidelines before students begin critiquing one another's work. Those guidelines will vary depending upon your particular goal for the class meeting. But here are some suggested directives that work well for students who are just beginning to learn how to respond to one another's writing. These can be written on the board or printed on a "Reader Response Form" and distributed in class for student use.

- State in your own words what you believe to be the central point of your classmate's paper.

- Write down, in order, the supporting details the writer uses to develop the central point.

- Was any passage (a word, phrase, sentence, paragraph) in your classmate's paper unclear to you? If so, place brackets around it.

- In one or two sentences, explain what you like most about your classmate's paper.

- Think of one or two changes or additions the writer could make to improve the paper. Write them down here.

As follow-up to the collaborative work, instructors can proceed in a number of ways. For instance, if our students have been working together on the activities following a reading selection, we sometimes re-assemble the class as a whole and ask a representative of each group to write responses to the exercises on the board, using the following format:

Maria's Group	Ronni's Group	Ed's Group	Damon's Group
1.	1.	1.	1.
2.	2.	2.	2.
3.	3.	3.	3.
4.	4.	4.	4.

After the students write their responses, we discuss the answers that are different, asking members of the various groups to explain their reasoning. Then, as a class, we discuss the reasons for eliminating incorrect answers and methods for arriving at the correct response. At other times, rather than re-convene as a class, we collect the responses of each group, correct them, and return them at the next meeting. It's possible also to have each group save its work in a manila folder and to hand it in every week or two for review.

When students share their writing in groups, we usually give them a few days to make revisions, use the writing lab, or see us during office hours or established conference periods. We then collect the revised paragraphs or essays (along with the classmates' responses) and make additional comments for revision and/or assign a grade. The collaborative process also works well during the revising phase, after we comment on and hand back a student's draft. Students can revise their papers and then bring them to the group for feedback before making final revisions and submitting them for a grade.

Conferencing

When time permits, we like to meet with our students for individual conferences. Just a few minutes of one-to-one discussion about an early draft of a student's paper can be far more effective than a page full of written comments (that the student might not even read!).

While it may be tempting to point out all the errors in a student's paper, we find it most helpful to focus on just one or two central problems. For example, a student may not have made a strong central point, or one section may contain a good deal of irrelevant material, or the paper may lack a pattern of organization. Students are easily discouraged when confronted with a barrage of criticism; they are best able to hear your comments (and most likely to actually learn from them) if you concentrate on just one or two problem areas. In your written comments on the paper, of course, you can indicate other places that need fixing. In our conferences, we try to balance our criticisms with comments on what the student has done well.

If you require students to hand in their rough drafts with their finished papers, and if you have your students keep folders of their work, you can easily track each student's development as a writer. Together, as the course continues, you can review how a student is overcoming a particular problem, or provide additional strategies if he or she continues to repeat old mistakes.

Individualized Work

Whole-class instruction, small-group collaborative work, and conferencing with the teacher are all valuable instructional tools. Ultimately, though, students need to become confident and reflective readers and thinkers in order to become active, independent learners. *Voices and Values* is designed to give students the essential independent practice they need to develop such skills.

One way we like to encourage students' individual work is by using the "First Impressions" questions that follow each reading selection. Because the questions ask for the students' most basic, "gut" reactions to what they have read, they lend themselves well to independent work. They are ideal for use as the basis for either in-class writing or journaling done outside of class. Through writing their responses to the "First Impressions" questions, students can deepen their own understanding both of a reading and of their own reactions to it. They can begin to explore the ways that their own experience and observations merge with or diverge from those of an author. Perhaps most importantly, they can begin to bridge the gap between reading and writing, realizing that through their own writing, they have the ability to enter into a dialogue with the printed word.

The two introductory chapters that precede the essays can also be used for individualized instruction. The book's first chapter, "Becoming a Better Reader," guides students step by step through each of the activities that follow the readings. The second chapter, "Becoming a Better Writer," is key to a student's understanding of the writing assignments he or she will encounter in the text. Students should work through each chapter thoroughly. We have recommended that instructors make those chapters the bases of the opening classes. In addition, you may wish to return to certain parts of these chapters (or recommend that students do so) on an as-needed basis as you, for instance, address a particular reading or writing technique or a step in the writing process. Whatever the case, students need repeated practice in the various vocabulary, comprehension, rhetorical, and organizing strategies addressed in the activities. They also need frequent feedback to check the accuracy of their thinking and to reinforce growth.

Finally, an answer key to the Vocabulary and Reading Checks for all the selections appears later in this *Instructor's Manual* (pages 9–18). The answer key allows instructors to score students' responses quickly, so that feedback can be immediate and direct. In addition, since the material in this manual is not copyrighted, instructors can photocopy the answer keys for students' independent use.

READABILITY LEVELS . . . AND THEIR LIMITATIONS

On the next page are the readability grade levels for the two introductory chapters of the book and the forty reading selections. Because *Voices and Values* has been prepared on a computer, and because several software programs provide readability statistics, it has been possible to do a complete readability evaluation for each reading, rather than merely sampling excerpts from the materials.

Please remember, however, that there are limits to the reliability and validity of readability scores. First of all, there are many different ways to measure readability, each using different criteria—and yielding different results. For example, here are the methods used by the three readability formulas that appear below:

- The **Flesch-Kincaid** score indicates the grade level of the document based on the number of syllables per word and number of words per sentence. This score predicts the difficulty of reading technical documents; it is based on military training manuals that score in difficulty from 5.5 to 16.3.

- The **Coleman-Liau** score indicates the grade level of the document based on the average number of letters per word and number of sentences per 100 words.

- The **Bormuth** score indicates the grade level of the document based on the average number of letters per word and per sentence. These scores indicate grade levels ranging from 6.3 to 11.6.

Second, a readability formula, as indicated above, is merely an accounting of the number of characters, words, sentences, and/or paragraphs in a piece of writing. It does *not* consider such significant factors as student interest in the subject of the piece, prior knowledge of the subject, the number of examples provided to explain concepts, and the overall clarity, logic, and style of the writing.

Thus, while "Responsibility" has a readability level of—depending on which measurement you prefer—5th, 6th, or 8th grade, it is a sophisticated adult piece that may be more challenging to students than, for example, "Thank You," which has a reading level of 9th, 14th, or 11th grade.

We respect readability levels, but we also take them with a grain of salt, and we have kept other factors in mind as we chose and sequenced the readings.

Material	Word count	Flesch-Kincaid grade level	Coleman-Liau grade level	Bormuth grade level
Becoming a Better Reader	3227	7.73	13.57	10.6
Becoming a Better Writer	4876	6.70	11.24	9.8
Unit One				
1. Bird Girl	1659	6.42	7.69	8.9
2. The Scholarship Jacket	1954	4.41	5.80	7.8
3. Life Over Death	1229	4.30	4.67	7.5
4. A Small Victory	1605	5.17	7.86	8.2
5. Joe Davis: A Cool Man	2227	4.97	7.58	8.2
6. From Horror to Hope	2056	6.73	6.97	8.5
7. Migrant Child to College Woman	3686	5.19	6.44	8.5
8. He Was First	2474	9.10	9.73	9.9
Unit Two				
9. Night Watch	658	6.16	8.21	8.9
10. Thank You	1639	9.23	14.68	11.20
11. Winners, Losers, or Just Kids?	738	9.87	10.84	10.1
12. Responsibility	719	5.52	6.33	7.8
13. Anxiety: Challenge by Another Name	1264	7.82	8.36	8.9
14. The Bystander Effect	1557	8.50	10.75	9.5
15. Don't Let Stereotypes Warp Judgments	1550	10.23	10.20	9.7
16. Dealing with Feelings	1659	9.41	15.3	10.9
Unit Three				
17. All the Good Things	1151	4.97	6.71	8.9
18. The Yellow Ribbon	925	4.60	9.31	9.2
19. What Do Children Owe Their Parents?	2240	6.46	8.70	9.2
20. Shame	1767	4.70	5.90	8.5
21. Rowing the Bus	2025	6.36	7.30	8.9
22. Bullies in School	1820	11.45	18.91	11.6
23 Seven Ways to Keep the Peace at Home	3155	8.97	10.99	10.1
Unit Four				
24. Dare to Think Big	1036	7.70	8.74	9.2
25. A Change of Attitude	2425	7.18	7.14	8.5
26. From Nonreading to Reading	1506	6.50	6.56	8.5
27. Reading to Survive	3507	5.35	7.18	8.9
28. Flour Children	975	7.30	8.43	8.9
29. In Praise of the F Word	951	7.39	9.36	9.2
30. The Professor Is a Dropout	3038	6.57	8.93	9.2
31. Learning Survival Skills	3346	7.33	8.31	8.9
Unit Five				
32. Tickets to Nowhere	706	5.94	7.46	8.9
33. An Electronic Fog	1005	6.68	8.35	8.9
34. The Quiet Hour	1024	8.10	12.82	10.6
35. Rudeness at the Movies	1196	7.36	10.27	9.5
36. My Daughter Smokes	1292	7.58	9.70	9.2
37. Here's to Your Health	1062	8.43	10.82	9.5
38. A Drunken Ride, A Tragic Aftermath	3322	7.27	10.31	9.5
39. Living the Madison Avenue Lie	1461	8.45	13.30	10.6
40. Staying Power	2902	5.72	8.85	9.2

A FINAL WORD

Voices and Values is a highly versatile teaching tool. Its range of engaging, thought-provoking readings, its emphasis on the fundamentals of effective reading and writing, and its generous number of assignments designed for a range of abilities and approaches make it easily adaptable to a wide spectrum of instructional goals and needs. We hope that your students will enjoy and learn from all that this book has to offer.

Answer Key

UNIT ONE

1. Bird Girl

Vocabulary Check

1. b	5. a
2. c	6. c
3. b	7. c
4. d	8. b

Reading Check

1. d	6. d
2. b	7. a
3. d	8. F
4. a	9. b
5. c	10. d

2. The Scholarship Jacket

Vocabulary Check

1. b	5. c
2. b	6. a
3. d	7. b
4. d	8. c

Reading Check

1. c	6. c
2. b	7. b
3. b	8. T
4. b	9. d
5. T	10. c

3. Life Over Death

Vocabulary Check

1. c	5. b
2. b	6. a
3. c	7. c
4. d	8. b

Reading Check

1. b	6. c
2. b	7. c
3. c	8. b
4. a	9. c
5. b	10. d

4. A Small Victory

Vocabulary Check

1. c	5. c
2. d	6. b
3. c	7. a
4. a	8. a

Reading Check

1. b	6. c
2. d	7. d
3. d	8. d
4. T	9. c
5. a	10. c

5. Joe Davis: A Cool Man

Vocabulary Check

1. c	5. b
2. a	6. a
3. b	7. a
4. c	8. b

Reading Check

1. b	6. b
2. a	7. c
3. c	8. a
4. c	9. d
5. a	10. b

6. From Horror to Hope

Vocabulary Check

1. a	5. b
2. c	6. a
3. c	7. c
4. c	8. c

Reading Check

1. b	6. F
2. a	7. d
3. b	8. a
4. b	9. a
5. a	10. c

7. Migrant Child to College Woman

Vocabulary Check

1. d	5. b
2. a	6. a
3. c	7. b
4. b	8. c

Reading Check

1. b	6. c
2. a	7. F
3. b	8. b
4. d	9. b
5. d	10. a

8. He Was First

Vocabulary Check

1. b	5. c
2. b	6. a
3. c	7. c
4. a	8. b

Reading Check

1. c	6. c
2. d	7. T
3. b	8. c
4. a	9. b
5. F	10. a

UNIT TWO

9. Night Watch

Vocabulary Check

1. d	5. c
2. b	6. c
3. d	7. a
4. c	8. b

Reading Check

1. b	6. d
2. d	7. a
3. a	8. a
4. d	9. c
5. c	10. b

10. Thank You

Vocabulary Check

1. b	5. b
2. d	6. b
3. b	7. c
4. d	8. b

Reading Check

1. b	6. a
2. b	7. d
3. d	8. d
4. c	9. d
5. a	10. b

11. Winners, Losers, or Just Kids?

Vocabulary Check

1. b	5. c
2. c	6. b
3. d	7. a
4. a	8. b

Reading Check

1. d	6. d
2. a	7. a
3. b	8. a
4. b	9. d
5. c	10. c

12. Responsibility

Vocabulary Check

1. b	5. b
2. a	6. c
3. d	7. a
4. a	8. a

Reading Check

1. c	6. a
2. d	7. a
3. d	8. a
4. c	9. b
5. b	10. c

13. Anxiety: Challenge by Another Name

Vocabulary Check

1. d   5. b
2. a   6. b
3. b   7. c
4. b   8. c

Reading Check

1. c   6. b
2. c   7. c
3. b   8. b
4. c   9. d
5. d   10. b

14. The Bystander Effect

Vocabulary Check

1. c   5. c
2. d   6. a
3. b   7. c
4. b   8. c

Reading Check

1. d   6. c
2. a   7. c
3. d   8. d
4. b   9. b
5. d   10. d

15. Don't Let Stereotypes Warp Your Judgments

Vocabulary Check

1. b   5. b
2. d   6. b
3. d   7. b
4. b   8. a

Reading Check

1. a   6. c
2. c   7. T
3. d   8. d
4. b   9. c
5. b   10. c

16. Dealing with Feelings

Vocabulary Check

1. b   5. b
2. d   6. a
3. c   7. c
4. a   8. c

Reading Check

1. b   6. F
2. d   7. b
3. a   8. b
4. a   9. c
5. c   10. b

UNIT THREE

17. All the Good Things

Vocabulary Check

1. b	5. a
2. a	6. c
3. b	7. b
4. c	8. c

Reading Check

1. b	6. d
2. c	7. c
3. b	8. a
4. b	9. F
5. c	10. b

18. The Yellow Ribbon

Vocabulary Check

1. c	5. a
2. a	6. c
3. b	7. c
4. a	8. a

Reading Check

1. d	6. c
2. b	7. b
3. d	8. c
4. b	9. c
5. b	10. c

19. What Do Children Owe Their Parents?

Vocabulary Check

1. a	5. b
2. c	6. b
3. a	7. a
4. b	8. b

Reading Check

1. a	6. d
2. a	7. T
3. b	8. c
4. T	9. c
5. c	10. d

20. Shame

Vocabulary Check

1. a	5. b
2. c	6. c
3. b	7. c
4. d	8. a

Reading Check

1. c	6. a
2. a	7. F
3. d	8. c
4. b	9. b
5. d	10. d

21. Rowing the Bus

Vocabulary Check

1.	c	5.	b
2.	b	6.	c
3.	c	7.	b
4.	a	8.	a

Reading Check

1.	c	6.	c
2.	a	7.	c
3.	a	8.	b
4.	d	9.	F
5.	a	10.	a

22. Bullies in School

Vocabulary Check

1.	b	5.	a
2.	a	6.	b
3.	c	7.	b
4.	b	8.	a

Reading Check

1.	d	6.	c
2.	a	7.	c
3.	b	8.	b
4.	F	9.	a
5.	d	10.	b

23. Seven Ways to Keep the Peace at Home

Vocabulary Check

1.	d	5.	c
2.	b	6.	a
3.	a	7.	b
4.	d	8.	b

Reading Check

1.	c	6.	d
2.	a	7.	c
3.	c	8.	c
4.	d	9.	a
5.	F	10.	c

UNIT FOUR

24. Dare to Think Big

Vocabulary Check

1. b	5. b
2. a	6. a
3. d	7. c
4. a	8. b

Reading Check

1. a	6. a
2. b	7. F
3. b	8. b
4. a	9. b
5. a	10. b

25. A Change of Attitude

Vocabulary Check

1. c	5. b
2. d	6. c
3. c	7. c
4. c	8. a

Reading Check

1. b	6. d
2. a	7. d
3. d	8. c
4. b	9. c
5. d	10. b

26. From Nonreading to Reading

Vocabulary Check

1. a	5. a
2. b	6. b
3. c	7. c
4. b	8. c

Reading Check

1. d	6. b
2. b	7. b
3. b	8. b
4. c	9. d
5. F	10. b

27. Reading to Survive

Vocabulary Check

1. a	5. b
2. c	6. c
3. d	7. a
4. d	8. a

Reading Check

1. d	6. c
2. b	7. T
3. a	8. c
4. b	9. d
5. b	10. c

28. Flour Children

Vocabulary Check

1. c	5. b
2. a	6. b
3. b	7. c
4. b	8. b

Reading Check

1. d	6. T
2. d	7. d
3. a	8. c
4. d	9. a
5. a	10. d

29. In Praise of the F Word

Vocabulary Check

1. a	5. b
2. c	6. a
3. b	7. b
4. a	8. c

Reading Check

1. d	6. a
2. c	7. c
3. c	8. b
4. c	9. F
5. b	10. d

30. The Professor Is a Dropout

Vocabulary Check

1. a	5. b
2. c	6. c
3. c	7. a
4. c	8. c

Reading Check

1. c	6. d
2. b	7. c
3. a	8. b
4. c	9. d
5. b	10. d

31. Learning Survival Skills

Vocabulary Check

1. b	5. a
2. c	6. a
3. d	7. b
4. c	8. b

Reading Check

1. b	6. d
2. a	7. c
3. b	8. d
4. c	9. c
5. a	10. c

UNIT FIVE

32. Tickets to Nowhere

Vocabulary Check

1. c	5. b
2. c	6. a
3. b	7. c
4. d	8. c

Reading Check

1. c	6. c
2. a	7. c
3. c	8. d
4. c	9. d
5. c	10. b

33. An Electronic Fog Has Settled Over America

Vocabulary Check

1. b	5. a
2. c	6. b
3. b	7. c
4. c	8. c

Reading Check

1. d	6. F
2. b	7. d
3. c	8. d
4. c	9. c
5. c	10. b

34. The Quiet Hour

Vocabulary Check

1. c	5. b
2. d	6. a
3. c	7. c
4. c	8. c

Reading Check

1. d	6. a
2. d	7. a
3. a	8. b
4. T	9. b
5. b	10. c

35. Rudeness at the Movies

Vocabulary Check

1. a	5. c
2. b	6. c
3. c	7. a
4. d	8. b

Reading Check

1. b	6. b
2. c	7. F
3. c	8. d
4. F	9. d
5. c	10. a

36. My Daughter Smokes

Vocabulary Check

1.	a	5.	c
2.	c	6.	a
3.	a	7.	b
4.	b	8.	b

Reading Check

1.	b	6.	F
2.	a	7.	a
3.	c	8.	b
4.	c	9.	b
5.	d	10.	d

37. Here's to Your Health

Vocabulary Check

1.	c	5.	b
2.	a	6.	c
3.	a	7.	b
4.	c	8.	b

Reading Check

1.	b	6.	c
2.	c	7.	d
3.	b	8.	b
4.	c	9.	F
5.	b	10.	c

38. A Drunken Ride, A Tragic Aftermath

Vocabulary Check

1.	a	5.	c
2.	b	6.	a
3.	c	7.	b
4.	b	8.	b

Reading Check

1.	a	6.	d
2.	a	7.	a
3.	c	8.	c
4.	a	9.	b
5.	F	10.	b

39. Living the Madison Avenue Lie

Vocabulary Check

1.	d	5.	c
2.	b	6.	a
3.	d	7.	b
4.	b	8.	a

Reading Check

1.	d	6.	c
2.	c	7.	F
3.	b	8.	c
4.	b	9.	d
5.	d	10.	a

40. Staying Power

Vocabulary Check

1.	c	5.	a
2.	c	6.	c
3.	a	7.	c
4.	c	8.	b

Reading Check

1.	b	6.	d
2.	c	7.	c
3.	b	8.	b
4.	d	9.	d
5.	c	10.	c

Suggested Answers to the Discussion Questions

UNIT ONE

1. Bird Girl

1. Many centuries ago the Greek philosopher Philo of Alexandria made the following observation: "Be kind, for everyone you meet is fighting a great battle." What do you think he meant by this statement? How might it apply to "Bird Girl"?

   Answer: Philo was probably referring to the fact that, without exception, each us is dealing with our own heartaches and disappointments in life. Even people who look as if they don't have a care in the world are struggling with their own secret fears. Philo is asking us to recognize that our fellow humans are wrestling with their own problems, and to treat them as gently as we ourselves would want to be treated. In the case of "Bird Girl," only the student who bravely came to her defense seemed able to empathize with the "great battle" the "bird girl" was fighting.

2. In paragraph 2, DeLeon says that "it's important when you're a teenager to join the laughter, lest the laughter turn on you." What does he mean? Is he correct?

   Answer: Teenagers, perhaps more than older people, tend to put a lot of value on being part of a group. They will sometimes do things they would not do on their own—even things they consider wrong—to be accepted by the larger group. Laughing at people the group considers different is one way of showing that a person is part of the group. If a teen won't laugh, he or she is showing that being part of the group isn't as important as something else—perhaps following his or her conscience. In revenge for leaving the group, the group may next laugh at him or her.

3. Why do you think so many readers wrote to DeLeon about the story of the Bird?

   Answer: For almost everyone, high school is a difficult time of, on one hand, trying to fit in, and on the other hand trying to establish one's own identity. Almost every present or former high-school student can identify with someone in "Bird Girl," either as a victim of bullying, a bully, or a person who allowed someone else to be bullied.

4. DeLeon asks, "How can we make teenagers treat each other like human beings?" How would you answer this question?

   Answer: Answers will vary, but here are some likely points for discussion:

   - Learning moral values at home or in church
   - Stories like those printed in DeLeon's column and/or television shows that point out cruelty and compassion
   - Teenagers daring to stand up for what they believe in rather than always going along with the crowd
   - Teenagers, parents, teachers, and others commending or rewarding courageous and considerate behavior
   - Having health, psychology, sociology, or ethics courses focus on teenagers' social and psychological problems and needs
   - Having schools, communities, and church groups provide various organizations and activities for teenagers to give teens membership in peer groups that share their interests

2. The Scholarship Jacket

1. In her first meeting with the principal, Marta could have challenged him by telling what she had overheard the two teachers saying. Why do you think she stayed silent? What do you think the principal would have said or done if she'd told him she knew the real reason she wasn't being given the jacket?

    Answer: There could be several reasons why Marta didn't tell the principal what she had heard. She may have been afraid of seeming disrespectful to the principal. She may have been afraid of angering him or the teachers. She may have felt a misplaced sense of shame over what she had heard. She may have felt it was taboo to talk to the principal about racism.

    The principal would surely have been worried and embarrassed if he knew what Marta had overheard. He might have denied it, claiming that Marta had misunderstood. He might have taken his anger out on her, accusing her of eavesdropping. Or he might have been so ashamed that he agreed to give her the jacket.

2. Why do you think the principal gave in during his second meeting with Marta? What do you think will happen when he has to face the Board again? If you were the principal, what would you say to the Board?

    Answer: The principal apparently recognized the truth of what Marta said—that if the jacket were paid for, it wouldn't be a scholarship jacket. He knew in his heart that Marta deserved the jacket.

    The principal will be in trouble with the Board. The members of the Board, which include Joann's father, apparently are more concerned with keeping the "important" people in the community happy than they are in recognizing true scholarship. The Board might even threaten the principal's job.

    Answers to the third question will vary, but it seems likely that the principal will tell the Board that as an educator, he has to see the scholarship jacket given to the student who has earned it.

3. What values did Marta learn from her grandfather? Where in the story do they demonstrate similar values?

    Answer: Marta seems to have learned several things from her grandfather: to work hard; to be dignified; and to do the right thing, even if it costs her. Marta has worked very hard to earn such good grades. She demonstrates dignity at several points in the story: when she looks the principal "straight in the eye" as he tells her she must pay for the jacket; when she stands "with all the dignity I could muster" to leave his office; and when, as she tells the principal she will not pay, she sits very straight in her chair and forces herself not to cry. She demonstrates her commitment to doing the right thing when, although she desperately wants the jacket, she admits to herself that her grandfather is right in refusing to pay for it.

4. Marta implies that she was discriminated against because of her racial background (she was Mexican) and her family's economic condition (they were poor). Have you ever experienced discrimination, or do you know of a friend who has experienced it? Explain.

    Answer: Answers will vary.

3. Life Over Death

1. In the first paragraph, the author uses the expression "death with dignity." What do you think he means by that expression?

   Answer: In this case, the author seems to mean that by moving the cat off the road, he is giving the cat the "dignity" of some privacy and more peaceful surroundings, rather than the noise and confusion of the highway, where its body would undoubtedly be hit again.

2. When the vet told Broderick that he could pick up his cat at the vet's office, the author began to protest but then stopped. Why do you think Broderick decided the cat was really his?

   Answer: He realized that, by making the decision to save the cat's life, he had become responsible for that life. It was up to him to make sure the cat now had a home.

3. Why do you think that Pokey has become, in Broderick's words, "our most beloved cat"? Do you think Pokey's injuries had an effect on how the author ended up feeling about him? Why or why not?

   Answer: Pokey sounds like a lovable animal, with his good nature and the "half-smile" on his face. But it is likely that his injuries made Broderick even more fond of him. Broderick probably took a special delight in seeing the badly injured cat become a playful, healthy animal. Broderick may even have felt that, in a way, he was "meant" to have Pokey, because of the way he and the cat encountered each other.

4. Can and should something be done to make the world a better place for hurt and homeless animals like Pokey? Or should our priorities lie elsewhere? Explain your answer.

   Answer: Some students may think that animal welfare should be a high priority, and that, for example, there should be more "no-kill" animal shelters. Others will say that, with all the human needs in the world, animal welfare is not important. Still others may say that while human welfare is most important, that a society that doesn't care about hurt and homeless animals is unlikely to care much about needy people, either.

4. A Small Victory

1. If Steve Lopez hadn't written about Mrs. Knight, what do you think might have happened to her? Do you think anyone else in the story would have continued to try to help her?

   Answer: The article reports that Mrs. Knight had already begun to ration her supply of Ensure Plus. Therefore, it is possible that, if Dr. Spiegel and Steve Lopez hadn't helped her, she would have slowly starved. She would probably have continued to lose weight until she either died or Dr. Spiegel was able to reinsert her feeding tube. This surgery and hospitalization would have cost much more than the $6 a day it took to feed Mrs. Knight without the tube.

   It seems likely that Dr. Spiegel would have continued trying to find a way to help her. Steve Lopez doesn't say, but it sounds as though it was Dr. Spiegel who contacted him and asked him to help publicize Mrs. Knight's problem. This would explain Lopez's publishing the doctor's telephone number at the end of the first article.

2. What do you think Lopez means when he says in paragraph 20 that Medicare has "built-in safeguards against intentional or accidental use of common sense"? What is Lopez implying by his choice of words?

    Answer: By writing that Medicare has "built-in safeguards against intentional or accidental use of common sense," Lopez uses sarcasm to criticize Medicare. He implies that Medicare's rules are unrealistic and do not serve the people they are meant to help. The words "accidental use of common sense" also imply that the people who work for Medicare are as likely to use common sense by accident as on purpose. From this statement, we can infer that Lopez views Medicare as an inflexible system so bound up by its bureaucratic rules that it is blind to the ridiculous situations its own rules sometimes create.

3. Lopez writes, "Medicare reasons that if you don't need a tube, you don't need a special diet. The rule exists to avoid abuse." What kind of abuse do you think Medicare might be trying to avoid by having such a rule? How might Medicare be taken advantage of by people who wanted to do so?

    Answer: The rule that Mrs. Knight had to struggle against must have been designed to deter people who would try to get Medicare to pay for supplies they really don't need. A person could abuse the Medicare system if, for example, he was able to eat a normal diet and yet continued to pretend he needed a liquid supplement like the one Mrs. Knight needed to survive. If he was successful, Medicare would pay for a product that he could then sell for his own profit.

    In dealing with this question, it might help students to discuss what they know about abuse of other government benefits, such as welfare or disability benefits.

4. Lopez writes, "People called for two reasons. Compassion and anger" (paragraph 54). Why do you think so many people reacted with such depth of feeling? What events have you read or heard about recently that provoked a similar response in you?

    Answer: People are often outraged to hear about innocent people being victimized. Mrs. Knight's situation provoked particularly strong feeling because, as a dignified woman who had worked all her life, she clearly deserved better treatment. Answers to the second question will vary.

5. Joe Davis: A Cool Man

1. When speaking of his suicide attempt, Joe said, "It wasn't the spinal cord injury that did it. It was the addiction." What do you think Joe meant? Why do you think he blamed his addiction, rather than his disability, for his decision to try to end his life?

    Answer: Although his injury was a serious one, it was less harmful to Joe's spirit and self-esteem than his addiction. As a partially paralyzed man, Joe could still learn to live a rich and positive life. But as an addict, his life could go nowhere but downhill.

2. Why do you think the students Joe spoke to laughed as he shared personal details of his life? Why did they later quiet down? What effect do you think his presentation had on these students?

    Answer: Many teenagers laugh when they are unsure how to react. They may have laughed if they felt embarrassment or were moved by Joe's words. As the first wave of uncertainty passed, however, it became easier for them to listen quietly to what Joe had to say to them. Joe helped the situation from becoming worse by not becoming upset or angry when the students laughed. Answers to the last part of the question will vary.

3. Joe speaks of wanting to "regain the trust of people he once abused." In other words, he hopes they will give him a second chance. Have you ever given a second chance to someone who had abused your trust? Alternatively, have you ever sought a second chance from someone you had wronged? What happened?

   Answer: Answers will vary.

4. Joe wants young people to learn the lessons he has learned without having to experience his hardships. What lessons have you learned in your life that you would like to pass on to others?

   Answer: Answers will vary.

6. From Horror to Hope

1. Can you understand why Phany's mother might not have supported her daughter's desire to continue her education? How did Phany's point of view regarding education differ from her mother's? Why do you think their views were so different?

   Answer: Although answers to these questions will vary, they may touch upon the different generations that Phany and her mother belonged to, as well as the traditional role of women in Cambodian society. Phany's mother had been able to survive only by doing hard physical labor. It must have been very hard for her to comprehend what value advanced education could have for her children. In addition, as Phany says, Cambodians have traditionally considered education for women unnecessary. In many societies, families invest in their sons' education, assuming that women need less education in their traditional roles caring for homes and children.

2. What were the actual reasons Phany's uncle wanted her to come to the United States? Why do you think he changed his mind and wanted to send her back to Cambodia?

   Answer: Apparently Phany's uncle wanted her in the U.S. to serve as a live-in servant for his family and business. One possible reason for his change of mind might be that Phany was more assertive than he expected, and he was unwilling to deal with her. Perhaps he even located another relative who wanted to come to America, but did not require him to pay college tuition.

3. Phany's job at her uncle's doughnut shop turned out to be a nightmare. What is the worst job you have ever had? What made it so terrible?

   Answer: Answers will vary.

4. What challenges have you faced in getting to college? Describe one or two obstacles and how you overcame them.

   Answer: Answers will vary.

7. Migrant Child to College Woman

1. Maria's children work in the fields, as their mother had. In what ways are those children's lives different from Maria's life when she was a child working in the fields?

   Answer: As a child, Maria was little more than a slave. She earned nothing from the work that she did. She was denied an education or any kind of normal home life. She was brutalized by her father. By contrast, Maria's children keep the money that they earn. They have a stable home life, are treated lovingly by their parents, and are encouraged to see education as a high priority.

2. Why might it have been so important to Maria to learn to read after her daughter began school? What do you think she imagined might happen if she did not learn to read?

   Answer: Maria was determined to provide a better life for her daughter than had been provided for her. She realized that she would be handicapped as a parent if she could not read well. If she did not learn to read, she probably feared both that her daughter would be ashamed of her and that her daughter might follow her example and not become well educated.

3. Why do you think Mrs. Seth cried upon reading Maria's narrative about giving phony excuses to her grade-school teacher? Why might Maria have thought that Mrs. Seth was disappointed with what she had written?

   Answer: Mrs. Seth was deeply touched to realize what Maria had gone through in order to have arrived in her class. So many bad things had happened in Maria's life that she had never developed much self-esteem. Especially because school was such a scary experience for Maria, it was probably easy for her to assume that she had done poorly.

4. What do you think Maria means when she says she wants to teach migrant children to "stand on their own two feet"? What do you think all children must learn in order to "stand on their own two feet"?

   Answer: As a child, because of her poverty, lack of education, constant moves, and fear of her father, Maria had little control over her own life. By helping to provide more education, self-esteem, and life-skills training to migrant kids, Maria hopes they will find it easier to guide their own lives in positive directions. Answers to the second part of the question will vary.

8. He Was First

1. Kellmayer writes, "By 1944, the social climate had become more accepting of integration, in large part because of the contribution of black soldiers in World War II." Why might the contribution of black soldiers in World War II have affected how people felt about integration in the United States?

   Answer: As the black soldiers who had fought bravely during World War II returned to civilian life, white Americans were forced to see them as fellow Americans to whom they owed gratitude and respect.

2. Why do you think the idea of integrating professional sports inspired such strong feelings in people? Would the integration of another profession—medicine or law, for example—have gotten people so excited? Why or why not?

> *Answer:* The integration of professional sports may have inspired such strong feelings because athletes are such public figures. The white public could ignore black doctors or lawyers. But people who attended sports events or read the national papers were forced to see black and white athletes playing together.

3. Do you think Branch Rickey was right to ask Robinson "not to fight back"? Was Robinson right to agree? Explain your answers.

> *Answer:* Answers will vary. Students may object to Robinson's pacifism as a sign of weakness, or as giving in to Rickey's desire to show Robinson as a "good Negro." They may believe that Robinson's right to defend himself outweighed Rickey's wishes. Alternatively, they may look at the outcome of Robinson's actions and defend his restraint as having been justified. They may point out that if Robinson had fought back, his actions, rather than the integration of the team, would have become the focus of attention.
>
> Students might wish to explore this question: How do you think the Jackie Robinson/ integration of baseball story would have been changed if Robinson *had* fought back against his tormenters?

4. Robinson had to face a great deal of racism. Unfortunately, despite greater integration today, racism still exists. Have you experienced any racial insults yourself or seen anyone else treated badly because of the racial or ethnic group he or she belongs to? Describe what happened and how you or the other person reacted.

> *Answer:* Answers will vary.

UNIT TWO

9. Night Watch

1. At what point do you think the Marine realized that the man was not his father? How can you tell?

> *Answer:* The Marine knew as soon as he saw the man that he was not his father. We know that because, after the man died, the Marine told the nurse, "I knew right off there'd been a mistake."

2. Why didn't the Marine immediately reveal that a mistake had been made? Do you think his decision was the right one? Why or why not?

> *Answer:* The Marine told the nurse that he had stayed silent because the old man needed his son, and his real son couldn't be there. Because the old man seemed to believe the Marine really was his son, the Marine didn't want to disappoint him. Answers to the second part of the question will vary.

3. If you had been the man's son, how might you have felt when you learned what had happened?

> *Answer:* Answers will vary. Many readers will feel that the real son would have mixed feelings—great gratitude for the Marine's kindness, jealousy of a stranger who spent crucial time with his father, and sadness at having been denied the opportunity to be with his father one more time.

4. The author refers to the "uniquely human way" in which the Marine showed "that there are people who care what happens to others." Have you seen other examples of people going out of their way to help strangers? What do you think motivates people to help people they don't know?

   Answer: Answers will vary.

10. Thank You

1. What did the three replies that Haley received have in common? Why do you think Haley was surprised by what they said? What did these replies teach him about human nature?

   Answer: Each of them thanked Haley for having taken the time to thank them. As well, each suggested that what he or she had done for Haley was nothing special. Haley was surprised because he clearly thought that each of the three people richly deserved his thanks. From their replies, Haley realized how deeply people hope that their efforts will be noticed and appreciated.

2. Do you ever write personal letters or e-mail? To whom? And do you, like Haley and his shipmates, enjoy receiving mail? Is receiving a letter or e-mail better than receiving a telephone call? Why or why not?

   Answer: Answers will vary.

3. Haley believes we need to say "thank you" more often. But most of us say and hear "thanks" many times a day. What's the difference between everyday "thank you's" and the kind of thanks that Haley is talking about? Give an example of each.

   Answer: Many "thank you's" are automatic and don't mean a great deal. For example, many of us automatically say "thanks" to a cashier who rings up our groceries. Haley is talking about much more deeply felt expressions of appreciation. Such a meaningful thank-you occurs, for example, when a student takes the time to visit a previous year's teacher and thank him or her for good teaching.

4. Haley urges readers, "Find the good—and praise it." Some people can do this easily; others cannot. Why do you think people might have difficulty expressing gratitude or praise? Do you experience this difficulty? Explain.

   Answer: People often say they feel embarrassed to express praise or gratitude. When we express such feelings, we are exposing ourselves emotionally. We feel safer—less emotionally vulnerable—when we act "cool" and untouched by feelings. The bad part of "playing it cool" is that we become more and more isolated from other people, as well as from our own feelings. We miss the opportunity to have the kind of meaningful exchange that Haley experienced with his father, teacher, and grandmother. Answers to the last part of the question will vary.

11. Winners, Losers, or Just Kids?

1. What does Wightman really mean by "winners" and "losers"? Why does the title also say, "or Just Kids"?

   Answer: By "winners" and "losers," Wightman is referring to how his classmates saw themselves when they were in high school. They judged themselves on the basis of how popular they were for a few brief years. Wightman describes winners as people who succeeded academically, were attractive, and had money. He describes losers as those who did poorly in school (spending more time "tuning cars and drinking beer" than studying) and socially, and who enlisted in the Army instead of advancing their careers by going to a university. By adding "or Just Kids" to the title, Wightman suggests that "winners" and "losers" are not as fitting terms as they at first may seem to be. The labels of "winners" and "losers" really meant very little. It was after high school that the students really began to develop their identities, and the "losers" often ended up on top.

2. What do the first two paragraphs of this selection accomplish? Why do you think Wightman chose to begin his essay with these instead of with the story of his fifteen-year reunion?

   Answer: Wightman describes the "winners" and "losers" in his own high school—and identifies himself as a loser—in order to show the reader how these two groups of students were identified. By describing them first as they were in high school, Wightman heightens the contrast with their very different status fifteen years later.

3. Since their high-school experiences were so negative, why might Wightman and Paula have decided to attend the reunion? Do you think you will attend your high-school reunion? Why or why not?

   Answer: As Wightman points out, "only happy and successful people" went to the reunion. *Because* their high school experiences had been negative, Paula and Wightman were probably all the more eager to let their former classmates know that, far from being losers, they had turned out to be happy and well-adjusted. Answers to the second question will vary.

4. Wightman and many of the people whose stories he tells have shaken their self-image as "losers." What does Wightman say are the reasons for this transformation? What are some other factors that might determine whether a person can change his or her self-image?

   Answer: Wightman suggests that some people are just "slow to get started"—what might be termed "late bloomers." He also refers to the valuable ability some people have to "overcome their mistakes, seize second chances and fight to pull themselves together, day after day." There is some suggestion that people who find it easy going early in life—the "winners"—may not develop those abilities as readily as the people who have had a harder time of it. Answers to the last part of the question will vary.

12. Responsibility

1. Peck refers to the "ludicrous"—that is, ridiculous—lengths people will go to to avoid taking responsibility for their problems. What do you think he finds ludicrous about the sergeant's behavior? The young wife's? Do you find their behavior ridiculous? Why or why not?

   Answer: Peck finds it ridiculous that the sergeant blames "this damn island" for "driving" him to drink rather than admit that he has a serious drinking problem. The young wife is ridiculous because although she whines about her loneliness and boredom, she will not take the simplest steps to improve her situation. Answers to the rest of the question will vary.

2. What problems—big or small—do you observe around you that result from people refusing to take responsibility for their own behavior?

   Answer: Answers will vary.

3. What do you think Peck means when he says that "we must accept responsibility for a problem before we can solve it"? Can you give an example from your (or someone else's) experience to illustrate the meaning of his statement?

   Answer: Peck means that a person must accept a problem as his or her own—rather than putting the blame for it on other people or circumstances—before being able to solve it. Answers to the rest of the question will vary.

4. Why do you think so many people find it difficult to take responsibility for their own problems? How might they be helped to do so?

   Answer: Answers will vary. Reasons for people's reluctance to take responsibility might include the following:

   • Laziness—it's just easier not to
   • Fear—a person may be afraid of taking responsibility and then failing or being in a new, unfamiliar situation
   • The lure of gaining sympathy from others by complaining about a situation, rather than trying to fix it.

13. Anxiety: Challenge by Another Name

1. Can you understand why Collier turned down the chance to go to Argentina? Would you have felt some of the same fears he felt? Explain.

   Answer: Answers will vary, but students may sympathize with some or all of the following fears: encountering a different culture, not knowing the language, being far from home and family. All these fears are natural, but they do close off opportunities for growth.

2. Do you agree with Collier that anxiety has a positive side? Can you give an example from your own life of a decision that has made you feel anxious, as opposed to a decision that has left you feeling depressed?

   Answer: Answers will vary.

3. The same situations that make some people anxious do not affect others at all. What are some particularly anxiety-provoking situations for you? Possibilities include speaking in public, meeting new people, eating alone in a restaurant, driving in an unfamiliar city. What strategies have you developed for dealing with your particular anxieties?

   Answer: Answers will vary.

4. Like most people, at one time or another, you have probably decided not to take on a challenge because it made you feel too anxious. How did you feel about yourself and your decision? In the long run, do you think the decision worked out for the best, or would you do it differently if you had another chance?

   Answer: Answers will vary.

14. The Bystander Effect

1. Have you ever been influenced by the bystander effect? What was the situation? How did you explain your own response?

>   *Answer:* Answers will vary.

2. In paragraph 31, the author writes, "Bystanders look to others for cues as to what is happening. Frequently other witnesses, just as confused, try to look calm." Have you seen examples of this happening? Why would people try to look calm during an emergency?

>   *Answer:* Answers will vary. People try to look calm during an emergency for several reasons. For one, they do not want to cause panic in others. But probably more often, they are afraid they will look foolish if they overreact to a situation that turns out to be less serious than it first appeared.

3. One witness to the Trenton rape said, "We thought, well, it might turn out to be her boyfriend or something like that." If the rapist had been her boyfriend—or her husband—should that have affected whether witnesses interfered? Why or why not?

>   *Answer:* Answers will vary. Teachers might take the opportunity to let students know that a man's personal relationship with a woman—being her husband or boyfriend—does not give him any more right to beat or rape her than a stranger would have.

4. Judging from your experience, are there ways other than those described in this article that people act differently in groups than they act when they are alone? What other effects can being in a group have on individuals?

>   *Answer:* Answers will vary.

15. Don't Let Stereotypes Warp Your Judgments

1. What are some of the stereotypes you have heard or seen in jokes, ads, movies, books, or television shows? Did you think they were stereotypes when you first encountered them?

>   *Answer:* Answers will vary. Although students may be reluctant to repeat jokes at the expense of certain groups of people, you might encourage them to do so, perhaps by telling one that you have heard. Ask students to identify the stereotyped person or group in the joke and to analyze the stereotyped attitude. Students may then want to share their own examples. Go on to discuss other, perhaps less obvious stereotypes in ads, movies, or TV shows. For example, what are some stereotypes in perfume ads, beer commercials, and clothing ads such as those for blue jeans? How are Californians, Southerners, Hispanics, and Italians stereotyped in movies and on TV? What dangers do these stereotypes pose to children who see them?

2. What stereotyped attitudes towards men and women have you come across? Are these stereotypes harmful in any way?

>   *Answer:* If students have difficulty with this question, you might ask about the following:
>
>   • Women talk too much; women gossip; men are uncommunicative
>   • Women are weak and frail; men act macho (but are afraid of blood)
>   • Women can endure pain better than men can
>   • Women are emotional; men are rational or cold
>   • Women like to be told what to do; men like to be mothered

Students might wish to explore these questions: How do these stereotypes lead to false expectations? How can these false expectations then lead to problems in school, the workplace, or relationships? How can they lead to learned helplessness?

3. What stereotypes do you find particularly harmful or offensive? What are some good ways to respond to people who reveal prejudiced or stereotyped attitudes?

> *Answer:* Answers will vary.

4. The author states, "Explore most prejudices (note that the word means 'prejudgment') and you will find a cruel stereotype at the core of each one." What do you think he means? How is a prejudice similar to a stereotype? How is it different?

> *Answer:* A prejudice has a stereotype at its core in this sense: In order to hold a prejudice—for example, against a particular ethnic group—one has to stop looking at the members of that group as individuals. Instead, one must rely on a negative stereotype—that all members of that group are lazy, dishonest, stupid, etc. A prejudice is like a stereotype in that they both are based on erroneous information and involve an unexamined belief about a person or people. But prejudice puts stereotypes into action. When you have a prejudice against a person, you allow the stereotype you hold of that person to influence how you think and act regarding him or her.
>
> Getting rid of prejudices would also undermine many stereotypes. Unfortunately, prejudices are sometimes deeply rooted emotionally and psychologically.
>
> Students might wish to explore this question: Is it possible that some people may be able to recognize their prejudices (even though they cannot completely overcome them) clearly enough to avoid making the mistake of stereotyping others?

16. Dealing with Feelings

1. What is the difference between describing feelings and displaying them? How might Doris describe her feelings (rather than displaying them) to Candy after Candy says, "That first paragraph isn't very well written" (paragraph 2)?

> *Answer:* Describing feelings involves *putting them into words* in a calm, non-judgmental way. Displaying feelings means *showing* them through words, movements, or expressions. Instead of displaying her feelings to Candy (by shouting angrily at her), Doris could describe her feelings by saying something like, "I feel really uncomfortable when you read over my shoulder like that. I'd rather you wait until I am ready to show you what I've written."

2. In paragraph 13, Verderber discusses "tactful" behavior, also known as "little lies." Do you think Verderber approves of these "little lies"? Why or why not?

> *Answer:* Verderber seems to disapprove of "little lies." He implies this by putting the words "tactful" and "little" in quotation marks, as if to suggest that being "tactful" is dishonest, and that "little" lies aren't so little.

3. Why do you think Verderber goes into more detail about describing feelings than the other two methods of dealing with feelings?

> *Answer:* Verderber spends more time dealing with describing feelings because he is recommending that as the best course of action.

4. What are some examples from your own experience of withholding, displaying, and describing feelings? How useful was each?

> *Answer:* Answers will vary.

UNIT THREE

17. All the Good Things

1. In this story, we read of two classroom incidents involving Sister Helen and her students. In one, she briefly taped a third-grader's mouth closed. In another, she encouraged junior-high students to think of things they liked about one another. In your opinion, what do these two incidents tell about Sister Helen? What kind of teacher was she? What kind of person?

   Answer: Both classroom incidents reveal Sister Helen as a sincere, well-meaning teacher. In the first incident, she is inexperienced; by the time of the second incident, she has become a skilled teacher with excellent judgment. In telling about the first classroom incident, Sister Helen shows her objectivity and lack of pride by saying of herself, "I made a novice teacher's mistake." Her action in taping Mark's mouth shut seems to embarrass her, but she feels she has to carry through on her promise. The second classroom incident involves a mature teacher who is able to judge her students' mood and instinctively react in a way that would accomplish her purpose, and more. Her decision to have the students write down nice things about one another demonstrates her desire to see her students enjoy school and appreciate one another, not merely learn their academic subjects.

2. Why do you think so many of Sister Helen's students kept their lists for so long? Why were the lists so important to them—even as adults?

   Answer: Most of us crave hearing good things said about us and treasure those compliments that we do receive. To have a whole list of good things that other people have said about us would be a rare and wonderful thing. Adults may *seem* less concerned with hearing good things about themselves than younger people, but inwardly their need to hear them is as strong as ever.

   Students might wish to explore this question: Do you remember something positive that was said about you years ago? How important was that comment to your self-image?

3. At the end of the story, Sister Helen tells us that she "cried for Mark and for all his friends who would never see him again." Do you think she might have been crying for other reasons, too? Explain what they might be.

   Answer: Sister Helen might have cried because she was touched to learn that something she had done—a "good thing" about *her*—had been so much appreciated by others. Sister Helen might also have been moved by the realization that her students had been in such need of appreciation.

4. "All the Good Things" has literally traveled around the world. Not only has it been reprinted in numerous publications, but many readers have sent it out over the Internet for others to read. Why do you think so many people love this story? Why do they want to share it with others?

   Answer: The story reminds readers of how much we all want and need the affirmation of others. Some people who read it are probably moved to get in touch with loved ones and let them know that they are appreciated. The sharing of Sister Helen's story may be an indirect way of reminding others to tell friends and relatives, especially young people, what "the good things" are about them.

18. The Yellow Ribbon

1. According to the information in the selection, what is Vingo's attitude toward his wife? What else do you learn about her at the conclusion of the story?

    Answer: Vingo clearly loves his wife and hopes that she will take him back, although he has left the decision up to her and expects the worst. While in prison, he wrote to her, "I understand if you can't stay married to me." He even suggested the possibility that she'd find "a new guy—she's a wonderful woman, really something." He has told her not to write to him and has even spared her the possible pain of seeing him again: if she doesn't want him back, all she has to do is *not* tie the yellow handkerchief to the tree. He shows "a cracked, much-handled snapshot" of his wife and family to the young people—further evidence of his love. From the way the story ends, we can infer that Vingo's wife is a warm, loving person who is generous in her ability to forgive whatever Vingo has done.

    Students might wish to explore this question: What might his wife's feelings have been upon learning her husband had to go to prison? Why might she not have written to him for three and a half years?

2. Why do you think the young people first became interested in Vingo? How do you think their attitude about him changed after they'd learned his story?

    Answer: At first, the young people are interested in Vingo because he seems so silent and alone. They imagine that there is some mystery or drama surrounding him. After they learn his story, they begin to care about him as a person who is risking a great disappointment. When they see the handkerchief-covered tree, they are overjoyed for him.

3. While there is much we don't learn about Vingo in this very short narrative, Hamill does provide us with clues to some important aspects of his personality. What evidence is there that he is a decent man, a person who we could feel deserves a second chance?

    Answer: Vingo doesn't make excuses for himself. He admits that he committed a crime and deserved to go to jail. He speaks of his wife with great love and respect. He makes it clear that he will not blame her if she chooses not to take him back. All these things indicate that Vingo has a great deal of good in him.

4. Many people are thrilled, some even to tears, by this story. How did you and your classmates react when you first read it? Why do you think "The Yellow Ribbon" has such a powerful effect on readers?

    Answer: Like the young people, the reader begins to care a lot about Vingo and his fate. He is at a turning point in his life, and what happens at the tree means a great deal in terms of both his past and his future. We all can empathize with anticipation of such moments. Hamill accents the drama of that moment by building up to it and saving it for last. This moment is especially meaningful because it represents that which we all seek—unconditional love. We all want to have someone ready to fill up a tree with ribbons of acceptance of us and to take us back into his or her life, no matter what mistakes we have made. We all want forgiveness and the right to a second chance.

19. **What Do Children Owe Their Parents?**

1. Which parts of Landers's advice do you agree with? Which letter (or letters) would you have answered differently? What advice would you have given instead?

   Answer: Answers will vary. But some students might disagree with Landers's primary assumption—that children owe their parents consideration, respect, and loyalty. If so, maybe the class needs to define these terms. What does Landers seem to mean by them? What do some of the class members mean by them?

2. Assume that you are a parent whose child has chosen a friend you do not approve of. How would you handle this situation?

   Answer: Answers will vary. Some students may have already faced such a situation, either as a parent or as a child. How was the situation handled? Perhaps the parent took a hard line and forbade the child to see the friend or limited their time together. Or maybe the parent told the child his or her misgivings about the friend and allowed the child to decide what to do. Or maybe the parent got to know the friend better and then acted on that broader knowledge.

   Students might wish to explore these questions: If they have faced such a situation, could it have been handled better than it was? How? What kinds of friends might a parent disapprove of?

3. What do you think college students living at home owe their parents?

   Answer: Answers will vary. College-age children are legally adults. Should they be subject to curfews or rules about visitors? To what extent should they help with household chores and expenses? (How might Ann Landers answer these questions?)

4. If you had children of your own, what do you think they would owe you? Why?

   Answer: Answers will vary. How many students, though, would agree in general with Landers's statement that children owe parents consideration, loyalty, and respect? And what do these terms *mean?*

20. **Shame**

1. Why do you think Gregory included both the classroom story and the restaurant story in his article? In what ways are the two incidents similar? What is the difference between the shame he felt in the first incident and the shame he felt in the second?

   Answer: The incidents illustrate that shame is something people can feel at different ages and under different circumstances. They are similar in that Gregory felt shame in both. They are different in the source of the shame Gregory felt.

   Had "Shame" not included the anecdote abut the wino, it would have focused on only one type of shame, that shame people feel when others look down on them, ignore their feelings, and feel sorry for them. The story about the wino introduces another type of shame. This type of shame—which Gregory felt when he "waited too long to help another man"—results when someone makes another person feel the first type of shame.

   The similarity between the two incidents is that in both cases someone has not taken another unfortunate person's feelings into account. The difference is that in the first anecdote, Gregory is on the receiving end of inconsiderate behavior, and the shame he feels is for something that is beyond his control. In the second incident, he is the inconsiderate one, and the shame he feels comes from his own failure to act. Gregory seems to be saying that the shame he felt in the second case was much greater.

2. We say that something is ironic when it has an effect that is the opposite of what might be expected. In this reading, Gregory uses irony in several places. In what ways are the following quotations from "Shame" ironic?

- "I never learned hate at home, or shame. I had to go to school for that."
- "If I knew my place and didn't come too close, she'd wink at me and say hello. That was a good feeling."
- "I looked at the wino with blood all over his face and I went over. 'Leave him alone, Mister Williams. I'll pay the twenty-six cents.'

"The wino got up. . . . He looked at me with pure hate."

Answer: We usually think of school as a place where children go to learn positive or useful things, not negative things like hate and shame. The irony in the first quotation is that school is meant to teach us something *better* than shame.

Gregory's "good feeling" was dependent upon his acting in a way that humiliated him. The irony in the second quotation is that we do not expect someone to feel good about knowing his "place" and keeping his distance.

It was too late for Mister Williams to "leave him alone." Gregory's belated offer to help him makes the wino hate him. The irony in the third quotation is that we would not expect a response that seems to be generous to be met with "pure hate."

3. Has anyone ever tried to help you in a way that embarrassed or hurt you, instead of pleasing you? If so, how did you feel toward that person? Explain.

Answer: Answers will vary.

4. The Community Chest incident could have had very different results if Gregory's teacher had handled the situation in another way. What do you think she should have done when Gregory said, "You forgot me"? Or could she have used a different method of collecting money from students? Explain.

Answer: The teacher could have called on Gregory. If she was concerned that he did not really have the money, she could have spoken to him quietly after class. Or she could have simply waited to see if he turned the money in or not, and if he did not have it, talk with him privately at that time. Also, there was no need to collect the money in such a public way. She could have had the children bring in their contributions without announcing them in class.

21. Rowing the Bus

1. Paul Logan titled his selection "Rowing the Bus." Yet very little of the essay actually deals with the incident the title describes—only the first and last paragraphs. Why do you think Logan chose that title?

Answer: Through his choice of title and by beginning with the rowing story and ending with a reference to it ("No one should have to row the bus"), Logan uses the image of rowing the bus to represent the cruelty and humiliation typical of situations involving bullies. "Rowing the bus" thus becomes a symbol of bullying of all sorts.

2. Logan wanted to be kind to George, but he wanted even more to be accepted by the other students. Have you ever found yourself in a similar situation—where you wanted to do the right thing but felt that it had too high a price? Explain what happened.

Answer: Answers will vary. Since bullies are everywhere, students are likely to have had experiences similar to Logan's. Thinking of bullies whom students have known may help jog their memories of relevant incidents.

3. Logan refers to "a sinister code of childhood that demands there must always be someone to pick on." What does the phrase "a sinister code of childhood" mean to you? Why do children need someone to pick on?

> *Answer:* Answers will vary, but students should consider the fact that picking on someone allows a bully to feel stronger and better than that person—in his own eyes as well as in others'. This fact suggests that at least some bullies have fundamentally weak self-images.

4. The novelist Henry James once said, "Three things in human life are important. The first is to be kind. The second is to be kind. And the third is to be kind." Are there things that teachers, school administrators, parents, and other concerned adults can do to encourage young people to treat one another with kindness rather than cruelty?

> *Answer:* Answers will vary. One possible response: In addition to acting kindly themselves, teachers can use reading materials and school incidents to initiate discussions and raise students' consciousness about kindness.
>
> Students might wish to explore this question: More specifically, what ways can you suggest to at least encourage young people not to bully? (Here are some things the schools can do to handle bullying: Use students and community volunteers to monitor playgrounds and lunchrooms and to help victims; provide martial-arts training to teach respect for others and self-confidence; institute a school policy making bullying an unacceptable offense. The next reading, "Bullies in School," offers additional insights and suggestions.)

22. Bullies in School

1. As a child, were you ever involved in bullying—either as the aggressor or as the victim? What effect did this involvement have on you? If you could live those years over again, would you do anything differently?

> *Answer:* Answers will vary.

2. How does, or how did, your school deal with bullying? After reading this article, what suggestions for stopping bullying would you make to your school?

> *Answer:* Answers will vary. Possible suggestions might include having "bullying awareness sessions" with students and teachers, to raise their awareness of the problem of bullying and its long-term consequences. Schools could enlist the help of student leaders to befriend children who were being bullied. Identified bullies and their parents could be brought into the school for counseling, and bullies could be warned of immediate consequences if their behavior continued. Bullies and victims could both be given training in problem-solving skills. Teachers and playground monitors could be instructed to notice and intervene in incidents involving bullying behavior.

3. Do you feel the job of controlling aggressive behavior in children should be left to the schools? How can others—parents, religious leaders, the larger community, and the media—be involved?

> *Answer:* If people in a neighborhood become acquainted with one another, through block parties, neighborhood watch programs, or just informal visiting, they develop some sense of responsibility for one another. As a result, they are more likely to become involved if they see a problem developing with a neighborhood child. Similarly, if a local church gets involved with neighborhood kids, perhaps through recreation programs, church leaders will have some relationship with local children and be more likely to become involved if they observe a child bullying or being bullied. Other community organizations—the police, the media—can try to become acquainted with local children before problems develop. If

children are isolated from their larger community, that community will shrug off the problem of bullying with the attitude "it isn't my child."

Students might wish to explore this question: From your observation, what kind of family and/or community situation produces children who bully? Or are some children just naturally aggressive, and the family and community don't make much difference?

4. Based on your own observations, what do victims of bullies seem to have in common? What could be done—at home, in the school, in the neighborhood—to help these children feel better about themselves and relate more easily to others?

   Answer: Answers will vary. Students should consider the fact that it often takes only one friend to make all the difference in a child's life. Being accepted by one other person often helps a lonely child get over his or her social awkwardness and develop better people skills.

23. Seven Ways to Keep the Peace at Home

1. As you were growing up, did you ever compare your own family to another family (real or imaginary) that you thought was more ideal? What are some ways that family was better or worse than your own family?

   Answer: Answers will vary. Students might wish to consider families they see on TV, which—since they are fictional—tend to function differently from those in the real world.

2. Who does Sugarman seem to believe is more to blame for family problems—parents or children? What examples from the selection support your answer? Do you agree with him? Why or why not?

   Answer: Sugarman suggests that parents are often to blame for family problems. He gives various examples in which although it was a child who was "acting out"—the hypochondriac little girl, the boy who been speeding, the girl who was using drugs and being promiscuous— upon examination, it became apparent that the children were just reflecting problems in the parents' lives. Answers to the latter part of the question will vary.

3. What are some negative ways that people in this selection got attention from other family members? Why do you think they behaved in the ways they did? How could they have gotten attention in less destructive ways?

   Answer: The little girl got attention by pretending to be sick. The teenage boy got attention by failing school, smoking pot, and speeding in his father's car. The teenage girl got attention by using drugs and becoming promiscuous. Mrs. Raymond got attention by developing physical ailments. They behaved that way because, like many of us, they didn't have the skills or the willingness to address the real problems. In each case, they might have been able to get attention by talking honestly about the things that were really bothering them.

4. Sugarman suggests seven strategies for creating peace at home. Can you think of another step that families could take in order to communicate better or reduce family tensions? Give an example of what happens when this step is not taken, and how the same situation would be affected if it were taken.

   Answer: Answers will vary.

UNIT FOUR

24. Dare to Think Big

1. It doesn't seem likely that Dr. Carson, a highly educated adult, often uses words like "cool" and "nerd" in his own conversation. Why, then, do you think he chose to use such language in his speech at Wendell Phillips High School? What effect do you think it had on the students?

    Answer: Dr. Carson was deliberately speaking in the language of students. He knew that one big reason high-school-age people have trouble being focused and thinking about the future is that they want to be considered "cool." He wanted students to think about the long-term consequences of being "cool" and being a "nerd." Answers to the last part of the question will vary, but undoubtedly Dr. Carson hoped his language would help students apply what he was saying to their own lives.

2. Do you tend to think much about your future and work towards future goals? Or are you more inclined to live for the moment, assuming that tomorrow will take care of itself? In your opinion, what are the advantages and disadvantages of each approach?

    Answer: Answers will vary, but here are some points students might raise: People who plan ahead are more likely to actually achieve their goals. They are more likely to find long-term satisfaction in their lives. One possible downside is that people who focus too much on the future might not develop the ability to appreciate the present. They might not enjoy the pleasures of being young. "Living for the moment," conversely, can be fun; people who live that way can devote themselves to having a good time. But that fun can turn to panic and self-criticism when the person realizes he or she no longer has the opportunities to get ahead that he or she once had.

3. Although Dr. Carson was a focused, committed student, he admits that peer pressure and his own hot temper sometimes got in the way of his success. What are some obstacles—internal and external—that stand in the way of your being the best student you can be? What are some ways you might overcome these obstacles?

    Answer: Answers will vary.

4. Dr. Carson speaks frequently to high school students because he has learned something about life that he believes can be of value to them. If you were asked to give a single piece of advice to a group of younger students, what would you say?

    Answer: Answers will vary.

25. A Change of Attitude

1. As Berry read self-help books, his attitude about himself and learning improved. In fact, reading those books eventually led him to go to college. Have you ever read a book that influenced the way you thought, acted, or felt about yourself? What was it you read and how did it affect you?

    Answer: Answers will vary.

2. Although Berry's father did not encourage him to go to college, Berry sees many good things about his dad. In what ways was his father a positive role model for him? From Berry's own actions as an adult, what valuable lessons might he have learned from his father's example?

> *Answer:* Berry's father was a good role model in the sense that he was a hard-working, responsible, honorable man who made his family's welfare a priority. As an adult, Berry has shown that he too is very hard-working (he works full-time as a meat-cutter while going to college). He cares about his family, obviously worrying that he doesn't give his wife and daughters the time and attention they deserve, but determined to set a good example for them.

3. Berry discusses some of the difficulties he faces as a result of being in college—struggling to find time to meet his obligations, giving up lawn care, spending less time with his family. If you are in college now, what difficulties do you face as a result of fitting college into your life? If you plan to go to college someday, what do you think will be some of the obstacles you might face?

> *Answer:* Answers will vary.

4. In closing his essay, Berry writes that at his college graduation, "there will be a celebration—a proper one." With what earlier event is he contrasting this graduation? Judging from how Berry describes himself and how he has changed, how do you think the two celebrations will be different?

> *Answer:* He is contrasting his coming graduation with his high school graduation, at which he got drunk, hit a stop sign, and ruined his clothes. It's likely that his college celebration will be alcohol-free and will genuinely celebrate his hard work and his family's sacrifices.

26. From Nonreading to Reading

1. Abbott's wife bought books for their baby daughter when the child was clearly too young to learn to read. In your opinion, can such a young child benefit from being exposed to books? If so, in what ways?

> *Answer:* Answers will vary, but students may say, among other things, that even babies can learn to associate books with pleasant, positive experiences. They can begin to realize the connection between printed and spoken words. They can learn to enjoy the repetition of favorite stories. The pleasure they take in being read to will translate into the pleasure of reading on their own.

2. Abbott identifies three factors that contributed to making him a nonreader: a lack of exposure to books as a child, little support for education from his family, and easy access to drugs and alcohol. Which of those three do you think had the greatest negative impact on him? Why? What are some ways parents can contribute to making a child a reader and a successful student?

> *Answer:* A case could be made for any of the three factors, but perhaps the lack of support for education would be the most difficult obstacle for a child to overcome. As Abbott grew up, he could have gotten access to books through school or a public library, and he could have chosen not to use drugs or alcohol, but he could not provide himself with a supportive home environment. A few ways parents can contribute to their children's success in school are by being readers themselves, by reading to their children, by showing an interest in their children's schoolwork, by becoming involved in their children's schools, by being in contact with their children's teachers, and by quickly intervening if they realize their children are having trouble in a particular subject.

3. Abbott started first grade with very little preparation for learning. As a result, his excitement about school soon turned to humiliation and disappointment. What do you think schools could do to help children like Abbott?

   Answer: Answers will vary. Students might mention any or all of the following: special courses, after-school help, counseling, special teaching techniques, and the like.

4. Throughout Abbott's life, people have humiliated him for being a poor reader. Why, then, do you think he has been willing to write this essay, letting countless other people know about his problem?

   Answer: Abbott knows from his own experience that embarrassment keeps many poor readers from seeking help. His desire to encourage those people has been stronger than his own embarrassment. He knows that hearing from someone who shares their problem— someone who has struggled, and succeeded, to learn to read well—will have a powerful effect on readers in a similar situation.

27. Reading to Survive

1. As a child, Ryan used books as a "lifeline" to escape his troubled home life. When you are troubled or stressed, what do you do to make yourself feel better? Does your "lifeline" work as well for you as books worked for Ryan? Explain.

   Answer: Answers will vary.

2. Ryan's favorite book when he was little was *The Five Chinese Brothers*. Later, he found a new favorite: *Charlotte's Web*. From what his story tells you, why do you think these two books appealed so much to Ryan? If you also had a favorite book when you were younger, why did you like it so much?

   Answer: It's likely that one reason Ryan liked those two particular books so much is that they both focused on unlikely heroes—a little boy, the youngest of all his brothers, and then a little pig. Both were heroes who didn't seem very powerful, yet triumphed over adversity by using their wits. Ryan, who was facing so much trouble in his life, probably hoped that he, too, would be able to triumph over the odds. Answers to the last part of the question will vary.

3. Ryan kept silent about the abuse going on in his home because he was so afraid of Larry. Which people could a child in a similar situation go to for help? How could those people help the child without making the situation worse?

   Answer: An abused child could confide in a trusted adult. Some possibilities would be a teacher, a friend's parent, a school counselor, a doctor, or a pastor. Those adults could in turn contact the police or a social service agency that investigates abuse cases. The professionals involved would quickly separate the abuser and child so that the abuser could not punish the child for telling.

4. "You have to learn from the past to build your future," Ryan says. What lessons has Ryan learned from the past? What lessons from your past could help you build your future?

   Answer: Probably the most important lesson Ryan has learned is that, no matter how difficult a person's life has been, he or she does not need to let those problems dictate the future. Ryan realized that it was up to him to create a better life for himself. He began to focus on a better future, rather than feeling trapped by his unhappy past. A second lesson Ryan has learned (from Larry) is how *not* to be a father, and it's clear that Ryan is a loving and supportive father to his children. Answers to the last part of the question will vary.

28. Flour Children

1. In what ways is a "flour baby" like a real baby? What can it teach teenagers about parenthood? What can't it teach about parenthood?

   Answer: The flour baby's size and weight are approximately like a real baby's. The flour baby is like a real baby in that the students must care for it or face unpleasant consequences. It can teach teenagers a little about what an endless job and heavy responsibility a baby represents. But it is not like a real baby in many ways. The teenagers do not need to provide it with food, medical care, or clothing. They do not need to bathe it, keep it clean, or figure out what to do when it cries. The consequences they face if they do not care for the baby— failing the class, having to call a funeral home, or receiving a larger flour sack—are not nearly as serious as the consequences of neglecting a real baby. A flour baby cannot teach the reality of parenthood—only, to an extent, the responsibility involved.

2. In your opinion, how big a problem is teen parenthood? Are teenagers, in general, capable of being good parents? Why or why not?

   Answer: Answers will vary, and will likely reflect the students' own environment. A few of the problems associated with teen parenthood are these:
   - Young women often end up as single parents.
   - Teenagers are rarely prepared to care financially for themselves and a baby.
   - Teens may not be able to afford childcare while they work, and so end up on welfare.
   - Teenagers may resent the time and attention a baby takes up, and take their frustration out on the baby.
   - Teen parents often cut short their own prospects for higher education or career preparation.
   - The children of uneducated, low-income teen parents often end up poor and badly educated themselves.

3. If you were asked to help design a high-school program aimed at lowering the rate of teen pregnancy for that school, what would some of your ideas be?

   Answer: Answers will vary, but students will probably mention sex-education classes that would discuss methods of avoiding pregnancy and of resisting peer pressure. Bringing in teenage parents of both sexes who were willing to frankly discuss their problems could be helpful as well.

4. Teen pregnancy is only one of the problems that high-school students face. What are some other issues that teenagers confront? What kinds of courses, similar to Mr. Valverde's, might help them deal with these problems?

   Answer: Answers will vary.

29. In Praise of the F Word

1. Do you know anyone who has failed or almost failed a course? What effect did the experience have on that person?

   Answer: Answers will vary.

2. Most people think of failing a course as a negative experience. Why, then, does Sherry call it a positive teaching tool? In what ways can the threat of flunking be positive for students?

   Answer: Sherry considers it a positive tool because it demonstrates confidence in a student's ability to learn the material. This contrasts with the common practice of passing students who haven't mastered basic skills, a practice that is excused "by saying kids can't learn if they come from terrible environments." Sherry obviously believes most students can learn and that passing them without their having learned basic skills "dooms them to long-term illiteracy." She thinks that passing a student along is, in the long run, a negative experience, because it implies that a student is not capable of doing good work.

3. Besides the threat of failure, what are some other ways that teachers can motivate students? What have teachers done to make you want to work harder for a class?

   Answer: Answers will vary. As Sherry implies in paragraph 4, a teacher's style is one important factor in gaining students' attention and getting them to work harder. The more interested a student is in a class, the harder he or she will probably work. Other ideas teachers have used include providing rewards for good work, such as praise and awards; bringing people with interesting careers into class to inform and motivate students; and using reading materials that are relevant to students' lives.

4. People often look back on their education and realize that some of the teachers they learned the most from were their strictest teachers. Who do you think you have learned more from, strict teachers or easygoing ones? Give examples to support your point.

   Answer: Answers will vary. A discussion on this question might benefit from first describing just what a strict teacher is. Some characteristics of strict teachers are providing challenging work, expecting students to do all assignments on time, and handing out good grades only for good work.

30. The Professor Is a Dropout

1. Lupe credits her fellow Hispanic students with being a great help to her in college. Is there anyone in your life—a teacher, family member, or friend—who has helped you through challenging times during your education? Explain what your obstacle was and how this person helped you to overcome it.

   Answer: Answers will vary.

2. Lupe found that her school responsibilities conflicted with her duties as wife and mother. What kinds of personal responsibilities have you had to juggle as a student? These may include a job, a difficult home situation, your social life, your extra-curricular activities, or anything else that poses a challenge to your academics. How have you balanced these obligations with your role as student?

   Answer: Answers will vary.

3. By the end of Lupe's story we see the serious mistakes made by those who called her "retarded" and her children "slow learners." Was there ever a time when you felt people misjudged you? What did they say about you that was wrong, and how did it make you feel? Explain how you reacted to their judgments—did you accept their remarks or did you fight to disprove them?

   Answer: Answers will vary.

4. Lupe is an outstanding example of a person who took charge of her life. Would you say that you have taken charge of your life? Describe how you have done so, or describe what you think you must still do to truly be the "architect of your own destiny."

    Answer: Answers will vary. Encourage students to recognize even small accomplishments along the road to "taking control." Help students realize as well that blaming other people or circumstances for one's problems may be temporarily satisfying, but that taking responsibility for one's own problems is ultimately the only way to solve them.

31. Learning Survival Skills

1. What do you think Coleman means in paragraph 17 when she says, "A lot of people are their own worst enemies"? Have you ever observed anyone seemingly getting in the way of his or her own success? Have you ever done it yourself? Explain.

    Answer: By saying that people are often their own worst enemies, Coleman means that people often set themselves up to fail. They don't believe that they can succeed at a task, and so they put little effort into it. They may sabotage their own efforts—by, for example, skipping classes, arriving late or unprepared, or letting themselves fall behind. When these behaviors catch up with them, they feel justified in abandoning the task, saying "I knew it wouldn't work." Answers to the second part of the question will vary.

2. According to Coleman, students should plan for a career that both interests them and offers future job opportunities. What type of career interests you, and why? What degree would help you enter that field? Do you have any idea what the job prospects in that field might be?

    Answer: Answers will vary. Students might want to check with a counselor to determine the job prospects in fields that interest them.

3. Coleman ends her introduction (paragraphs 1–2) by stating, "Here, then, are my secrets for survival in college and, really, for survival in life as well." She then makes five points: "Be Realistic," "Persist," "Be Positive," "Grow," and "Enjoy." Which of those points represents the biggest challenge for you right now? Why?

    Answer: Answers will vary.

4. Although the author encourages students to make practical career plans, she also writes, "People should take some courses just for the sake of learning and for expanding their minds in different directions." What are some courses you would like to take "just for the sake of learning"? What about them appeals to you?

    Answer: Answers will vary.

UNIT FIVE

32. Tickets to Nowhere

1. Do you know anyone who, like Jim Oakland, depends more on luck than on hard work or ability? In what ways is this person like or unlike Jim? Do you respect the person? Why or why not?

   Answer: Answers will vary.

2. Suppose that five years from now, you could have $500,000. How would you feel about yourself if you had earned that money? Would you feel any differently about yourself if you had won it—say, in a lottery? Explain your answers.

   Answer: Answers will vary.

3. The story about Jim Oakland suggests that he never dates the same girl for very long. From what you know about Jim, what do you think are some possible reasons that he has a difficult time maintaining a relationship with a girlfriend? What do his choices concerning the lottery suggest about the kind of boyfriend or husband he would be?

   Answer: Jim doesn't seem like a man with much maturity or common sense. Although he dreams of being rich, he hasn't prepared himself for any kind of career. He is barely able to support himself, but he daydreams about buying a luxury car. He dropped out of school, supposedly in order to get rich, but instead he lived with his parents and didn't work at all. Instead of using his small salary wisely, he spends a large portion of it on lottery tickets. All of these things suggest that Jim would be an impractical, undependable boyfriend or husband. Most women would see Jim as a liability in their lives, rather than an asset.

4. As you read the selection, did you think that Jim would win the lottery, or that he would lose? What about the way Rooney wrote the selection made you think that?

   Answer: Rooney does seem to suggest that Jim will win the lottery. He deliberately builds up the suspense before the lottery drawing. He keeps emphasizing that although people laughed at Jim and his "system," Jim knew in his heart that he would win. He says Jim "had that lucky feeling." Students who were fooled might consider that if they imitate Jim's approach to life, they will be denying themselves the chance to be true winners.

33. An Electronic Fog Has Settled Over America

1. Do you agree with the argument that television makes people less intelligent and more passive? Why or why not?

   Answer: Answers will vary. Students who agree might mention how easy it is to simply watch whatever's on or to lazily channel-surf, or to let the shallow coverage of issues in TV news replace the more extensive and thoughtful discussions in a newspaper or newsmagazine. Students who disagree might cite programs that are truly educational: in-depth news specials, travelogues, entertainment shows that actually provide new insights and that increase their understanding of the world.

2. Are there other reasons you can think of for the steady fall in SAT scores since 1950? What are they?

> *Answer:* Answers will vary. Perhaps in 1950 going to college was unusual enough that a small percentage of well-prepared students took the SAT, whereas now, college has become a more accessible goal for many American families and a larger percentage of the population is taking the test. Students may also bring up the theory that SAT questions are biased against members of ethnic minorities and women.

3. As you were growing up, how much television did you and your family watch? Was the TV on most of the time, or did you and your family watch TV only when a special program was on? What, if any, restrictions were put on your TV watching?

> *Answer:* Answers will vary.

4. Based on your answers to the previous question, explain how you will deal with television in your home if you become a parent (or, if you already are a parent, how you do deal with it). How will your attitude toward TV be similar to or different from that of your parents? What, if any, restrictions will you (or do you) put on your children's TV watching? Explain.

> *Answer:* Answers will vary.

34. The Quiet Hour

1. What were family evenings like in your home as you grew up? Which did they resemble more: those described in paragraph 1 of the reading or those described in paragraph 2?

> *Answer:* Answers will vary.

2. How many hours a day do you watch TV now? If you cut down your viewing time by an hour or so a day, how do you think you would use that time? What activities might you do—or do more of?

> *Answer:* Answers will vary. (You might want to point out that Americans watch, on the average, more than seven hours of television a day.) Students could mention as possible activities to replace TV any of the following: reading, exercise, spending more time with family or friends, working part-time, volunteering, hobbies or extracurricular activities.

3. In order to make their argument stronger, authors often raise possible objections against it and then point out the weaknesses in those objections. What objections does Mayer raise to his own thesis, and how does he show the weaknesses of these objections? (See paragraphs 12–15.) Do you agree with him? Why or why not?

> *Answer:* Mayer states at first that television is an integral part of American life, and that he makes his living through TV. He refutes those arguments by claiming that TV has damaged children intellectually; that it has made them passive; and that it has weakened their political judgment. Answers to the rest of the question will vary.

4. Mayer writes, "With time to kill and no TV to slay it for them, children and adults alike might discover reading." He suggests one way to help children learn to enjoy books: by having parents read aloud to them. What are some other ways that parents could help their children enjoy reading?

> *Answer:* A few suggestions: By reading for pleasure themselves, parents can provide a powerful example to their children. They can make going to the public library and picking out books a pleasant family outing. They can make a family project of reading a book together, then seeing a movie based on the book and comparing the two.

35. Rudeness at the Movies

1. Do you agree with the author's theory about why some people are rude at the movies? What might be some other causes for this behavior?

   Answer: Answers will vary. Some students might think that Wine exaggerates, but is the spirit of his exaggeration accurate? Students might wish to explore these questions: Have any students ever complained in a movie theater because of others' rude behavior? Have any walked out or demanded their money back? Have any ever been asked to be quiet or leave the theater?

   Wine offers good reasons for people's rude behavior at the movies, and his emphasis on TV as the primary culprit appears sound. What are some other causes of rude behavior, though? For instance, do parents irresponsibly leave young children unattended in movies while they go shopping? Do some movies actually encourage audience reaction? Should theaters more strictly enforce age limits for R-rated movies?

2. Certain movies seem to bring out the worst in people. Which ones? Why?

   Answer: Answers will vary. Some movies that might fit this description include comedies whose humor is (to some) embarrassing or gross, suspenseful "Gotcha!" horror movies, *Rambo*-like action-adventure dramas, rock-concert movies, and poorly-acted erotic films.

3. Wine uses humorous exaggeration to make many of his points. For example, he claims that the man in front of him is "an inch or two taller than the Jolly Green Giant." Find other examples. Do you think this technique is effective, given the subject matter of Wine's essay?

   Answer: Answers will vary, but students should find plenty of material in the first twelve paragraphs: the drawbridge hairdo, "Essence of Elk," the Cub Scouts' noisemaking, the couple who want to tell the plot of the movie before it even starts—all part of the author's dream. Answers to the second question will vary.

4. In what activities besides moviegoing do you frequently observe rude behavior? What is the effect of such behavior on other people?

   Answer: Answers will vary. Rudeness can make life harder in any setting—at home or work, in class or at the supermarket, on the highway or in the parking lot. Often rudeness not only causes a breakdown in order (such as a person breaking into line, interrupting others, or parking illegally), but also causes a negative response in other people, usually anger or resentment. These feelings, at least for a while, dominate all others, causing physiological responses such as increased heartbeat and adrenaline excretion, which in turn lead to verbal or physical reactions against those who are rude. At the least, rudeness causes inconvenience and a loss of concentration. At the worst, it leads to retaliation, sometimes—road rage is an example—even violence.

36. My Daughter Smokes

1. What would you do if you had a friend who was involved in self-destructive behavior, such as smoking, excessive drinking, or drug use? Would you ignore the behavior? Would you try to persuade the friend to stop the behavior? What would be the risks of either choice?

   Answer: Answers will vary.

2. It's clear that smoking is a health hazard. Study after study shows that smoking leads to a variety of diseases, including cancer, emphysema, and heart disease. It has also become clear that second-hand smoke—smoke that non-smokers breathe when they are around smokers—is dangerous as well. If you had the power to do so, would you make smoking illegal or put any legal restrictions on smoking? Or do you believe that smoking should continue to be an individual's right? Explain.

   Answer: Answers will vary.

3. What is a bad habit of yours that you have tried to break? How successful were you? What made breaking that habit difficult?

   Answer: Answers will vary.

4. Suppose that you had a sixteen-year-old son or daughter. What rules would you expect him or her to obey while living in your home? Would you, for example, have a curfew for your child? Would you allow him or her to smoke in your home? How would you respond if you learned that he or she was drinking, using drugs, or becoming sexually active?

   Answer: Answers will vary.

37. Here's to Your Health

1. Dunayer presents and then refutes four false ideas about alcohol. What are these four ideas? According to Dunayer, what is the reality behind each? To what extent do you agree or disagree with Dunayer?

   Answer: The first false idea is that alcohol is connected with professional success. Dunayer says it is far more frequently connected with the lack of success. Second false idea: Alcohol makes you more sexually attractive. Dunayer says alcohol actually reduces sex hormones and causes infertility and impotence. Third false idea: Alcohol and sports go together. Dunayer says that alcohol dulls the reflexes and makes one physically incapable. Fourth false idea: Alcohol unifies families. Dunayer says that alcohol is to blame for many family problems. The extent of students' agreement or disagreement with Dunayer will vary.

2. If it's true that "beer doesn't make anyone sexier," why do you think so many young people drink so much beer in social situations? What are they hoping to achieve?

   Answer: Answers will vary, but one likely reason is that alcohol reduces people's inhibitions, which may make them feel more relaxed and flirtatious. They may also want to be viewed by others as cool, sophisticated, and able to "hold their liquor."

3. Think about a wine, liquor, or beer ad you have seen in a magazine, in a newspaper, or on television. What part of the alcohol myth described in "Here's to Your Health" does that ad promote? What details of the ad contribute to that element of the myth?

   Answer: Answers will vary.

4. Cigarette advertising is no longer allowed on television. Do you think beer ads should also be outlawed on TV? Should cigarettes and/or beer ads be banned from newspaper and magazines, too? Why or why not?

   Answer: Answers will vary.

38. A Drunken Ride, a Tragic Aftermath

1. The authors write in paragraph 14: "'I thought I was in control,' Baxter said. 'I wasn't driving like a nut; I was just . . . driving.'" What does this tell us about the effects of alcohol on drivers?

   Answer: One of the effects of alcohol is to give people a false sense of well-being and confidence, as if nothing can go wrong. A consequence is that drunk drivers often believe—wrongly—that they are not impaired.

2. To what extent do you think Tyson Baxter was responsible for the accident? Do you feel his passengers also were at fault in any way? If so, to what extent were they also responsible? Is there anyone else that you think is partly to blame for the accident?

   Answer: Answers will vary, but students may point out that the passengers had been drinking as well, and they chose to get into a vehicle with a driver they knew had been drinking. The passengers, too, were "swaying and rocking" the vehicle. They may think the blame is shared by the hosts of the drinking party and even the people who sold beer to the boys (although the boys used false identification). Most people, though, feel that by agreeing to be the driver, Tyson accepted responsibility for the other boys' safety.

3. What do you think would be an appropriate punishment for Tyson Baxter? If you were the judge in his case, what sentence would you give him? Why?

   Answer: Answers will vary.

4. Why do you think that, even after knowing what had happened to Tyson Baxter and his friends, some of his classmates would brag about their plans to "drink very heavily" during senior week? What, if anything, do you think could change those students' attitudes about drinking?

   Answer: Answers will vary.

39. Living the Madison Avenue Lie

1. Do you feel that your attitudes towards sex and intimacy have been influenced by television, the movies, ads, and commercials? Explain.

   Answer: Answers will vary.

2. Did you ever attend a sex-education class? What did it teach? What *didn't* it teach? What changes would you have made to improve the course? If you didn't attend such a class, do you think you missed something important? Explain.

   Answer: Answers will vary.

3. In arguing against the emphasis on sexuality in our culture, Garity focuses on potential dangers to young women. How do you think our highly sexualized culture affects young men? Are they also at risk? Explain.

   Answer: Answers will vary. Students may discuss the pressure on young men to "score," as well as the glamorization of male role models who have many sexual partners. Such sexualized media images give little encouragement to young men to establish loving, respectful relationships; to share responsibility for contraception; or to take equal responsibility for the children they father.

4. As Garity shows, the media and other influential parts of our culture often glamorize casual sex and sexual excess. Is there anything that parents can do to counteract that influence on their children? What could other authority figures or organizations do to help young people develop a healthier, more balanced view of sexuality?

   Answer: Answers will vary.

40. Staying Power

1. Would you call this story primarily a sad one or a happy one? What is sad about it? What parts of it could be called happy?

   Answer: Answers will vary. Many students will probably call the murder of Mr. Lee and Mrs. Lee's subsequent grief sad, but the coming together of the community and people's individual efforts to help a happy thing.

2. This article mentions that many corner groceries are being run by Korean immigrants. Where you live, are certain businesses run mainly by people from one country? What are those businesses, and who runs them? What reasons can you think of that certain businesses might attract specific ethnic groups?

   Answer: Answers will vary.

3. The murder of Mrs. Lee's husband was a crisis that pulled the surrounding community together. Have you seen a problem or crisis pull together people in your family or community who were not previously closely connected? What was the problem? Who responded to it, and how?

   Answer: Answers will vary.

4. Unfortunately, severely depressed neighborhoods like West Parkside are common within American cities. What factors do you think go into destroying a once-healthy community? Who is to blame? What, if anything, can be done to undo the damage?

   Answer: Answers will vary, but students may mention the moving of factories to countries where labor is cheaper, the flight of educated people to the suburbs, the influence of drugs and gang warfare, or the damaging effect of welfare dependence on people's sense of initiative.

Guided Writing Assignments

Note: The ten assignments that follow are expanded versions of assignments that appear in the book itself. Instructors wishing to provide additional guidance and examples for students to follow are encouraged to photocopy these pages for student use.

1   BIRD GIRL

Assignment

Write your own paragraph about a person who was teased or bullied in your school or neighborhood. Describe the person and then explain how others treated him or her. Make your description detailed enough so that your readers can picture the person clearly and understand what happened. Use a topic sentence such as "Gordon was teased a lot by my eighth-grade classmates because of his unusual behavior."

Prewriting

Spend ten minutes or so making a list of everything you can remember about your classmate and how he or she was teased or bullied. To get your thoughts flowing, ask yourself questions like "What did my classmate look like? How did he or she act? When did we tease the person most? How did we tease this person? How did he or she react?"

Here is a sample of one writer's list for a classmate named Moran Park:

— Korean features were unusual to us—darker skin, eyes were different
— Didn't speak English well, had a heavy accent
— Average height
— She was chubby
— We called her "Moron"
— We imitated her accent
— She had a friend named Lucy
— When we teased her she got excited and her accent and English got worse
— One time she yelled "Bad childs" at us and we laughed more

Review your list and cross out items that seem irrelevant. For instance, the facts that Moran was of average height and had a friend named Lucy do not add to the reader's understanding of her as a victim of bullying—therefore, the writer should cross those facts out.

How to Proceed

a. Remember that this paragraph, like all paragraphs, must have a main point. The main point generally appears at the beginning of the paragraph. A good main point for this paragraph could be "Moran Park was a target of teasing at our school because she was so different from the majority of kids."

b. Now write a first draft of the paragraph, organizing it in an order appropriate to the subject. For instance, the writer of this paragraph might organize the material by describing, first, what Moran looked and sounded like; second, how classmates teased Moran; and third, how she responded to that teasing. Here's the first draft of this paragraph:

I guess we teased Moran Park mostly because she was so different from the rest of us. Her dark skin and slanted eyes seemed unusual to us. She didn't speak English well at all. She often couldn't understand what was said to her, and her accent was so heavy that we had trouble understanding her. Kids responded to Moran in various cruel ways. We called her "Moron" instead of Moran. When she would try to speak English, we would imitate her accent and laugh at how she sounded. Sometimes someone would go into class early and draw a cartoon on the board and label it "Moran the Moron." When Moran got teased, she would become very excited and angry. She would shout at the people teasing her. Her English would become worse than ever at such times. I remember one time she yelled at a group of us, "You are bad childs!" and we just about fell down laughing.

c. Finally, re-read your paragraph and revise it as necessary. Notice if you need to add transitions, such as "for instance," "another reason," "instead," or "even though" to tie your thoughts together. Add or delete details as appropriate, check your spelling and punctuation, and consider adding a stronger opening point or concluding statement. Before you start revising, it can be very helpful to read your paragraph aloud. You are more likely to notice clumsy spots in your paper when you hear them read aloud than when you are just reading them silently. Here is our student-writer's final draft. New material is shown in **boldface** type.

~~I guess we teased~~ **Moran Park was a girl who was teased at my school**, mostly because she was so different from the rest of us. **She was Korean and most of us were white, so** her dark skin and slanted eyes seemed unusual to us. **She was also overweight. Another difference was that** she didn't speak English well at all. She often couldn't understand what was said to her, and her accent was so heavy that we had trouble understanding her. Kids responded to Moran in various cruel ways. We called her "Moron" instead of Moran. When she would try to speak English, we would imitate her accent and laugh at how she sounded. Sometimes someone would go into class early and draw a cartoon on the board**, showing a very fat Asian girl with slanty eyes and a pointed peasant hat,** and label it "Moran the Moron." When Moran got teased, she would become very excited and angry. She would shout at the people teasing her**, but unfortunately** her English would become worse than ever at such times. I remember one time she yelled at a group of us, "You are bad childs!" and we just about fell down laughing.

2   THE SCHOLARSHIP JACKET

Assignment

This story contains several examples of authority figures—specifically, the two teachers, the principal, and Marta's grandfather. Write an essay describing three qualities that you think an authority figure should possess. Such qualities might include honesty, fairness, compassion, and knowledge, among others.

Devote each of the supporting paragraphs in the body of your essay to one of those qualities. Within each paragraph, give an example or examples of how an authority figure in your life has demonstrated that quality.

You may write about three different authority figures that have demonstrated those three qualities to you. Alternatively, one authority figure may have demonstrated all three.

Your thesis statement might be similar to one of these:

- My older brother, my grandmother, and my football coach have been important authority figures in my life.

- My older brother's honesty, courage, and kindness to others have set a valuable example for me.

Prewriting

Before you begin writing your actual essay, spend some time thinking about your topic and writing down ideas you might include in the essay. For example, a student who wanted to use the second sample thesis statement might proceed like this:

<u>Thesis statement:</u> My older brother's honesty, courage, and kindness to others have set a valuable example for me.

<u>When</u> and <u>how</u> has my brother shown himself to be honest?

- In high school. Late writing a research paper, somebody showed him a website where he could buy a paper . He wouldn't do it.

- Last summer. Denise away for a whole summer, friends kept inviting him to go out with them to pick up girls. He didn't.

- Recently. Guy asked him to help him shoplift. Joel could have split profits. Said no.

<u>When</u> and <u>how</u> has my brother shown himself to be courageous?

- Last year. Neighbor man beating up his wife. Joel got involved, helped woman.

- Through high school. Volunteered at soup kitchen.

<u>When</u> and <u>how</u> has my brother shown himself to be kind to others?

- In the last few years. Never gets impatient when Grandma repeats herself.

- At college. Helps freshmen get adjusted.

Look through your list and decide which details you want to include in your essay and which ones aren't worth keeping. For example, the author of this essay realized she had more items for "honesty" than for the other two characteristics, so she decided to discuss Joel's honesty last of all in the essay. (The final point in an essay is generally the one your reader will remember, so you should try to make it an especially strong one.) She also realized that the item under "courageous" about volunteering in a soup kitchen did not really demonstrate a sense of courage. She decided to replace it.

How to Proceed

a.   Decide on a thesis statement. Your thesis should be one single sentence that clearly indicates what your essay will be about. Each paragraph in your essay will help to support that thesis statement.

b.   Decide on an organizational pattern that is appropriate for your subject. In this case, the writer revised her thesis statement to reflect the organization her essay would take:

>   My older brother's courage, kindness, and honesty have set a valuable example for me.

By writing *courage, kindness,* and *honesty,* the writer alerts the reader that she will be discussing the characteristics in that order. As noted before, she has saved her most important point for last.

c.   Write a rough draft of your paper. As you write, do not be tied too closely to the details written in your prewriting phase. If other good ideas occur to you, feel free to include them. Don't be too concerned yet with things like spelling and punctuation. You can edit and revise your material later. Here is our student's first draft:

>   Everyone needs someone to look up to. In my case, my older brother's courage, kindness, and honesty have set a valuable example for me.
>
>   Joel has always seemed like a courageous person to me. When I was little and some playground bullies were bothering me, he made them stop. Of course they were only nine and he was twelve so I guess he didn't have to be too brave to do that. Last summer we heard our neighbors having a fight, the guy was flipping out and then we begun to hear crashes and the lady screaming and begging the man to stop, like she was getting hit. All our neighbors were saying, "Oh, isn't that awful," but nobody did anything about it. Then Joel went to the people's door and banged on it until the man answered. He told Joel to mind his own business, but Joel told him he was going to call the police if the lady didn't come out. She came out and Joel asked her if she wanted to go to the hospital. She said yes and he took her there. That seemed like a very brave thing to me.
>
>   Joel is a kind person. My grandpa died four years ago. He was a really kind person, too. Since my grandpa has passed on, my grandma hasn't been doing too good. When you talk to her she tells the same stories over and over, mostly about when she was a little girl in Mississippi. She don't remember that she's told them to you like a million times before. It can get really borring and annoying after a while. But Joel always listens to her and he doesn't get impatient. Sometimes, if she's feeling sad and confused, he'll even say, "Tell me about when you were a little girl, Mom-mom." It always helps make her feel better when she can tell those old stories.
>
>   Once, when Joel was taking a high school history class, he was really late in getting started on a big research paper. He wanted to do well in the course. Then a friend of his told him about a website online where he could buy a research paper already written. He could pass it off as his own work. But Joel wouldn't do it. He started working hard on his own paper. He couldn't get it done in time, and he did get a lower grade for turning it in late. But he told me later, "I'd be ashamed to get an 'A' that I knew I hadn't earned." Another example of Joel's honesty happened last summer. Denise got a job down South so she could spend the summer with her relatives. Her mother lives in the same city as us, but she spent a lot of time with her aunts and uncles when she was growing up. He didn't see her for more than two months. All that time, his friends tried to get him to go out with them to pick up girls. They kept telling him Denise would never know. But Joel had promised not to step out on Denise, and he wouldn't ever go with them. Another really honest thing that Joel did was he refused to get involved in a shoplifting plan with one of his old buddies. Joel works nights at a department store, and the other guy had it all figured out how Joel could let him in threw an employee's entrance, grab some electronic equipment that Joel had put there, and then sell it and split the profits with Joel. Joel really got ticked at the guy. He didn't only tell him no, but he told him never to come into the store again while Joel was there.
>
>   All in all, I think my brother is a really courageous, kind, and honest person.

d. If possible, lay your essay aside for a day or two so that you can get a little distance from it before you begin revising. Then, re-read it critically, asking yourself the following questions:

— Have I included a clear thesis statement—one that accurately indicates the main idea of my whole essay?

— Does every one of my supporting paragraphs support that thesis statement?

— Does every one of my supporting paragraphs begin with its own topic sentence?

— Does every detail within a paragraph support that topic sentence? Or is there irrelevant material that needs to be *deleted*?

— Is the support of any of my paragraphs skimpy? Do I need to *add* more details?

— Do I need to correct errors in spelling, punctuation, or grammar?

— Is my language too slangy or informal?

— Have I used transitions between sentences and between paragraphs to tie my thoughts together?

— Have I written an effective introductory and concluding paragraph?

After reviewing her work with these questions in mind, our student-author produced the following revised essay. New material appears in **boldface** type.

Everyone needs a hero. My older brother, Joel, is mine. Joel's courage, kindness, and honesty have set a valuable example for me.

Joel has always ~~seemed like a~~ been courageous. ~~person to me.~~ When I was little and some playground bullies were bothering me, he **charged over like an angry bull and** made them stop. ~~Of course they were only nine and he was twelve so I guess he didn't have to be too brave to do that.~~ **As he grew up, he continued to be brave.** Last summer ~~we~~ **our whole neighborhood** heard our neighbors having a fight. ~~the guy was flipping out and then we begun to hear crashes and~~ **There were crashing noises** and the lady **was** screaming ~~and begging the man to stop, like she was getting hit~~ **as if she was getting hit.** ~~All our neighbors were saying, "Oh, isn't that awful," but nobody did anything about it.~~ **Nobody did anything about it—except Joel.** ~~Then Joel~~ **He** went to the people's door and banged on it until the man answered. He told Joel to mind his own business, but Joel told him he was going to call the police if the lady didn't come out. She came out ~~and Joel asked her if she wanted to go to the hospital. She said yes and he took her there~~**. and Joel drove her to the emergency room.** That seemed like a very brave thing to me.

~~Joel is a kind person.~~ **Not only is Joel courageous, but he is kind.** ~~My grandpa died four years ago. He was a really kind person, too.~~ Since my grandpa ~~has~~ passed on **four years ago,** my grandma hasn't been doing too ~~good~~ **well.** ~~When you talk to her~~ She tells the same stories over and over, mostly about when she was a little girl in Mississippi. ~~She don't remember that she's told them to you like a million times before. It can get really boring and annoying after a while.~~ ~~But~~ **Instead of getting annoyed or impatient,** Joel always listens to her. ~~and he doesn't get impatient.~~ Sometimes, if she's feeling sad and confused, he'll even say, "Tell me about when you were a little girl, Mom-mom." It always helps make her feel better when she can tell those old stories.

Finally, Joel is about the most honest person I've ever known. Once, when ~~Joel~~ he was taking a high school history class, he was really late in getting started on a big research paper. He wanted to do well in the course. Then a friend of his told him about a website online where he could buy a research paper. ~~already written. He could pass it off as his own work~~. But Joel wouldn't do it. He started working hard on his own paper. He couldn't get it done in time, and he did get a lower grade for turning it in late. But he told me later, "I'd be ashamed to get an 'A' that I knew I hadn't earned." Another example of Joel's honesty happened last summer. **Joel's girlfriend** Denise got a job down South so she could spend the summer with her relatives. ~~Her mother lives in the same city as us, but she spent a lot of time with her aunts and uncles when she was growing up.~~ He didn't see her for more than two months. All that time, his friends tried to get him to go out with them to pick up girls. They kept telling him Denise would never know. But Joel had promised not to step out on Denise, and he wouldn't ever go with them. Another really honest thing that Joel did was he refused to get involved in a shoplifting plan with one of his old buddies. Joel works nights at a department store, and the other guy had ~~it all~~ figured out ~~how~~ **that** Joel could let him in ~~threw~~ through an employee's entrance, grab some electronic equipment that Joel had put there, and then sell it and split the profits with Joel. Joel really got ~~ticked~~ **angry** at the guy. He didn't only tell him no, but he told him never to come into the store again while Joel was there.

I think I'm fortunate to have such a brave, kind, and honest brother. Whenever I'm tempted to do something wrong, I think of his example. I want Joel to be as proud of me as I am of him.

3   FROM HORROR TO HOPE

Assignment

Both in Cambodia and in Houston, Phany encountered cruel people. Write a paragraph in which you describe a cruel person you have known. In it, be sure to provide specific details that illustrate the person's cruelty.

Prewriting

One way to generate ideas for a writing project is to just "freewrite" for a few minutes. Freewriting is just what it sounds like: writing without any rules. Keeping your topic in mind, just write everything that comes into your head for ten minutes or so. Don't worry about spelling, punctuation, organization, or even whether what you are writing will be of any use. The simple act of writing can help you discover what you have to say about a topic.

One student working on the assignment above came up with the following piece of freewriting:

> Cruel sounds like a wicked stepmother in a fairy tale. do I know anybody cruel. the word cruel begins to look funny when you keep writing it. cruel cruel cruel. cruel spelled backwards is leurc. Hurting puppies and kittens is cruel. hurting little things that can't fight back. stomping on bugs. can bugs feel? Do bugs think? My paragraph: Do Bugs Think. You can be bad but not cruel— cruel is when they can't fight back. Cruel = hurting things like babies or little kids. A creepy woman used to live on our street with all the kids. Name was Elaine Irene Eleanor something like that? Whoa that's been a long time ago. something was really bad about her. they were scared of her. Me too. Didn't want to be near that house. Cold cold eyes. Did she ever smile? So quiet but not nice quiet. Scary quiet. Kids always had bruises and cuts on them. Did she do that? They were home sick a lot. I saw them look out of the windows. They always seemed scared.

By the time the student was finished with her freewriting session, she was filled with memories of a cruel woman who used to live in her neighborhood. She knew that she had a topic for her paragraph.

How to Proceed

a. Based on the ideas you've generated through freewriting or some other prewriting technique, develop a topic sentence, one that expresses the main idea of your paragraph. The student in our example came up with this:

> When I think of the word "cruel," I remember a woman who lived in my neighborhood many years ago.

With this topic sentence, the writer signals the reader that (1) her paragraph will be about the woman, and (2) it will show that the woman was cruel. *Every detail in the paragraph* should help fulfill the promise of the topic sentence.

b. Begin to write a first draft of your paragraph. Although you will probably use details generated in your freewriting, do not feel that they are *all* you should include. Other valuable ideas will occur to you as you write, and you should use them if they seem appropriate. You can always remove them later if you want.

Here is the first draft of the student's paragraph:

> When I think of the word "cruel," I remember a woman who lived in my neighborhood many years ago. Her name was Irene or Elaine or something like that. I never actually saw her do anything cruel. But even though I was just a little kid, I sensed her cruelty. We had a lot of children in the neighborhood. She lived in a red-brick house with yellow shutters on

the windows. She had a lot of kids. I don't know where their father was, or if they had different fathers. There were three that I played with sometimes, but there were older ones and babies too. I remember them as being thin, pasty-faced little kids who always had cuts and bruises all over them. They were never allowed in my house. When I invited them to come inside, they would just say, "She wouldn't like it." When we played together in the park, they acted like noisy, normal kids. But as soon as I got near their house (I never went into their house) they seemed to turn into ghosts. One creepy thing I remember is that when their mother wanted them to come in, she didn't call them. She would just stand in the doorway, looking at them. She had the coldest eyes I've ever seen. As soon as they noticed her watching them, the kids would hurry into the house. They wouldn't even say goodbye. Once, I remember Joanie didn't come out to play for what seemed like weeks. When I finally saw her, I asked where she had been. She looked at the ground and whispered, "I couldn't play because I was bad." I never heard their mother yell at them, and in a way that was the scariest thing of all about her. Ordinary mothers yell sometimes. But she was silent. The only time I remember hearing her voice was when I invited the kids to my birthday party. I didn't want to go to their door, so I waited until she came out on the porch. I walked up to her and asked if they could come. I remember the kids looking at the ground as I asked. She smiled in a nasty way and said, "I don't think so." Then they all went into the house. On the day of the party I remember seeing Joanie looking out the window. Soon after that they moved away.

c.   Read and revise your paragraph. Better yet, ask a fellow student to read it and insert his or her comments. Another reader can point out rough spots, missing details, a lack of transitions, or irrelevant material that you yourself might not notice. Based on written comments from another student, our writer revised her paragraph several times to come up with the following final version. New material appears in **boldface** type.

When I think of the word "cruel," I remember a woman who lived in my neighborhood ~~many years ago~~. **when I was about six.** ~~Her name was Irene or Elaine or something like that.~~ I never ~~actually~~ saw her ~~do anything cruel.~~ **hurt anybody.** But even though I was ~~just a little kid~~ **very young**, I sensed ~~her~~ **deep cruelty in her.** ~~We had a lot of children in the neighborhood. She lived in a red brick house with yellow shutters on the windows. She had a lot of kids. I don't know where their father was, or if they had different fathers. There were three that I played with sometimes, but there were older ones and babies too.~~ **I played with three of her many children. No father was in sight.** I remember them as being thin, pasty-faced little kids who always had cuts and bruises all over them. **They were kept home from school a lot, and they would say they were sick.** They were never allowed in my house. When I invited them to come inside, they would just say, "She wouldn't like it." **I didn't have to ask who "she" was.** When we played together in the park, they acted like noisy, normal kids. But as soon as we got near their house, they seemed to turn into **scared, silent little** ghosts. One creepy thing I remember is that when their mother wanted them to come in, she didn't call them. She would just stand in the doorway, looking at them. She had the coldest eyes I've ever seen. As soon as they noticed her watching them, the kids would hurry into the house. They wouldn't even say goodbye. Once, I remember Joanie, **the one closest to my age**, didn't come out to play for what seemed like weeks. When I finally saw her, I asked where she had been. She looked at the ground and whispered, "I couldn't play because I was bad." ~~I never heard their mother yell at them, and in a way that was the scariest thing of all about her. Ordinary mothers yell sometimes. But she was silent.~~ The only time I remember hearing ~~her~~ **the woman's** voice was when I invited the kids to my birthday party. I didn't want to go to their door, so I waited until she came out on the porch. I walked up to her and asked if they could come. I remember the kids ~~looking~~ **staring** at the ground as I asked. She looked at them **with a cold little smile and** ~~smiled in a nasty way and~~ said, "I don't think so." Then they all went into the house. On the day of the party I remember seeing Joanie looking out the window. Soon after that they moved away. **I hadn't thought of that woman for years, but when I do now, I feel goosebumps rising on my arms.**

4 THANK YOU

Assignment

Most people, Haley writes, "go about yearning in secret for more of their fellows to express appreciation." Select three categories of people who you think deserve more appreciation than they generally receive. Write an essay in which you explain, for each category, why these people deserve thanks and how the people whose lives they affect could show appreciation. Some categories of people you might write about are these:

- Parents
- Teachers
- Waiters and waitresses
- Store clerks
- Police officers
- Cleaning people
- Church volunteers
- School volunteers

Prewriting

You might generate ideas for this assignment with an exercise like this one. Select one category of people you think you might write about—for instance, waitresses. Then complete the following sentence in as many ways as you can: "Waitresses deserve appreciation because . . ."

A list of responses might look like this:

— They don't make much money.
— They are on their feet all day.
— They have to listen to the same stupid music all day.
— They have to carry heavy trays of food.
— They make a low hourly wage and have to depend on tips.
— They aren't responsible for the food, but they get all the complaints.
— They have to deal with rude customers.
— Some of them have to wear silly-looking uniforms or hats.
— They have to deal with drunk customers.
— They have to deal with customers' bratty kids.
— They have to deal with customers who walk out without paying.
— They have to deal with customers who make offensive suggestions.

As you look over your lists of ideas, see if several of them can be grouped within one larger category. For example, the list above could be divided up this way: (1) the physical difficulties of being a waitress, (2) the financial difficulties of being a waitress, and (3) the customer-related difficulties of being a waitress.

Now do the same for each of the other categories of people you are considering writing about. Keep going until you have substantial lists of ideas (at least six or seven ideas) for three categories of people. You will then know you have ample material to write the first draft of your paper.

How to Proceed

a. For each of the categories of people you are going to write about, make a simple outline like this:

1. Waitresses deserve appreciation.
   a. They work hard physically.
   b. They don't make much money.
   c. They have to put up with all kinds of difficult customers.

You will do the same for the other two groups you are writing about; for example, kindergarten teachers and school janitors.

b. Formulate a thesis statement that mentions each of the categories of people you will be discussing, like this:

Three groups of people in our society who deserve more appreciation than they get are waitresses, kindergarten teachers, and school janitors.

c. Once you have your thesis statement written and your outline done, you are ready to write a rough draft of your essay. After each of your points—such as "Waitresses work hard physically"—add specific details or examples that support that point.

Here is a rough draft of one such essay:

Three groups of people in our society who deserve more appreciation than they get are waitresses, kindergarten teachers, and school janitors.

Waitresses work very hard. They spend their entire day on their feet, walking from the kitchen to customers' tables. Their feet get tired and sore by the end of the day. They have to carry heavy, food-laden trays to the tables, then carry away trays full of dirty dishes that are almost as heavy. All this carrying is hard on their backs. Waitresses also have a difficult job money-wise. Most restaurants pay waitresses a lousy hourly wage. In order to make a decent salary, waitresses have to work very long hours and rely on customers' tips. Nobody gets rich being a waitress. Waitresses have to put up with all kinds of difficult customers. Customers yell at them if they don't like the food, even though the waitresses didn't cook it. Drunk customers make passes at them, and others sneak out without paying their bill. Families come in with bratty kids who run around the restaurant and spill things, and the waitress is expected to clean up after them.

Another group that deserves more appreciation than they get is kindergarten teachers. First of all, kindergarten teachers have a lot of responsibility. Secondly, kindergarten teachers sometimes don't get much support from the children's parents. A teacher can try her hardest to teach a child his numbers, letters, and colors, but if the child's parents aren't reinforcing that teaching at home, the child isn't going to learn very quickly. A lot of people aren't really well prepared to be parents, in my opinion. Kindergarten teachers have to deal with children who are very different in terms of their emotional development. Some kindergarten students are pretty mature and ready for school, but others are really just babies. They cry and can't concentrate on school activities, and the poor teacher has to deal with them.

School janitors are a final group who should be appreciated more. A janitor's work is never done. He can scrub the school floors and clean the lockers until they shine, but the next day they all get as dirty as ever. The janitor has to deal with students' worst characteristics. A teacher may see a student as being smart, or a good writer, or a fine athlete, but to the poor janitor, he's just another slob who drops things on the floor and writes on the wall. Finally, a janitor gets little respect from the students. People brush by him in the hallways as though he were a piece of furniture. Sometimes nasty kids will deliberately drop stuff right where he's working. Nobody seems to appreciate his work in keeping the school clean.

d. If possible, put your essay away for a day or two. Then re-read it carefully, asking yourself these questions:

— Have I included a strong thesis statement?
— Does every one of my supporting paragraphs begin with its own topic sentence?
— Does every detail within a paragraph support that topic sentence?
— Does every one of my paragraphs contain enough support?
— Do I need to correct errors in spelling, punctuation, or grammar?
— Is my language too slangy or informal?
— Have I used transitions between sentences and between paragraphs to tie my thoughts together?
— Have I written an effective introductory and concluding paragraph?

After being revised with these questions in mind, the final draft of the essay looked like this. New material is indicated in **boldface** type.

Three groups of people in our society who deserve more appreciation than they get are waitresses, kindergarten teachers, and school janitors.

Waitresses deserve appreciation for several reasons. For one thing, waitresses work very hard **physically**. They spend their entire day on their feet, walking from the kitchen to customers' tables. Their feet get tired and sore by the end of the day. They have to carry heavy, food-laden trays to the tables, then carry away trays full of dirty dishes that are almost as heavy. All this carrying is hard on their backs. **In addition,** waitresses ~~also~~ have a difficult job ~~money-wise~~ **financially**. Most restaurants pay waitresses a ~~lousy~~ **low** hourly wage. In order to make a decent salary, waitresses have to work very long hours and rely on customers' tips. Nobody gets rich being a waitress. **Finally,** waitresses have to put up with all kinds of difficult customers. Customers yell at them if they don't like the food, even though the waitresses didn't cook it. Drunk customers make passes at them, and others sneak out without paying their bill. Families come in with bratty kids who run around the restaurant and spill things, and the waitress is expected to clean up after them.

Another group that deserves more appreciation than they get is kindergarten teachers. First of all, kindergarten teachers have a lot of responsibility. **It's up to them to make sure that a child gets off to a good start in school.** Secondly, kindergarten teachers sometimes don't get much support from the children's parents. A teacher can try her hardest to teach a child his numbers, letters, and colors, but if the child's parents aren't reinforcing that teaching at home, the child isn't going to learn very quickly. ~~A lot of people aren't really well prepared to be parents, in my opinion.~~ **Most importantly,** kindergarten teachers have to deal with children who are very different in terms of their emotional development. Some kindergarten students are pretty mature and ready for school, but others are really just babies. They cry and can't concentrate on school activities, and the poor teacher has to deal with them.

School janitors are a final group who should be appreciated more. ~~A~~ **One reason is that a** janitor's work is never done. He can scrub the school floors and clean the lockers until they shine, but the next day they all get as dirty as ever. **A second reason is that** the janitor has to deal with students' worst characteristics. A teacher may see a student as being smart, or a good writer, or a fine athlete, but to the poor janitor, he's just another slob who drops ~~things~~ **candy wrappers** on the floor and writes **his girlfriend's name** on the wall. Finally, a janitor gets little respect from the students. People brush by him in the hallways as though he were a piece of furniture. Sometimes nasty kids will deliberately drop ~~stuff~~ **a soda on the floor**, right where ~~he's working~~ **he has just finished mopping**. Nobody seems to appreciate his work in keeping the school clean.

Our society is full of people who work hard to provide important services and who deserve appreciation for the work they do. Waitresses, kindergarten teachers, and school janitors are some of those people we should all take time to thank.

5   WINNERS, LOSERS, OR JUST KIDS?

Assignment

As Wightman suggests in this article, school is often a difficult, frustrating experience. What factors make school hard for so many people? Write an essay in which you isolate several kinds of pressures that, in your experience, make school so unpleasant. You might, for instance, write about one of the following:

- Pressure to conform
- Pressure to be part of a particular group
- Pressure to get good grades
- Pressure to be popular
- Pressure to have a boyfriend/girlfriend
- Pressure to look/dress/act in certain ways
- Pressure from parents

Prewriting

You may want to do some freewriting to prepare for this essay. When you freewrite, give yourself an assigned block of time—at least ten minutes—during which you write down anything that comes into your head about your topic. Spelling, punctuation, grammar, and even logic don't matter as much as simply continuing to write. When you cannot think of anything to write, write the word "freewrite" until another thought comes to you. For many people, simply starting to write is the hardest part. Once they are doing the act of writing, the ideas begin to flow.

Here is a sample of one student's freewriting about the pressures of high school:

> High school is tough. Parents don't understand how tough. Seems like everyone tries to be someone they're not. You gotta be this you gotta be that. Gotta be an athlete, gotta be a good student, gotta have a girlfriend, gotta be popular, gotta party, gotta try drugs, gotta hang out, gotta study, gotta gotta. freewrite freewrite its like you never can be just you. freewrite clothes and shoes are a big issue. suddenly everybody has one kind of basketball shoe and if you don't you're a loser. Loser! Everyone's greatest fear. Always trying to prove you're not a loser. what's a loser anyway? who makes up these rules? why do I care what some gym rat says is cool because he's got bigger biceps than me. Bodies, now theres a high school topic. Girls think they have it bad because they're supposed to be thin and all. it's bad for guys too. If you're short and skinny forget it. What a zoo! It's like school is this place you go to learn to feel bad about yourself. freewrite freewrite freewrite teachers and parents want you to care about classes. but to be cool you're suposed to act like you don't care about any of that. but the grades come out and I care then.

How to Proceed

a. Look over your freewriting and see if you notice particular kinds of pressure that you can develop in your essay. Our student writer identified several: the conflicting expectations of adults and students; the need to not be identified as a loser; the pressure to look a certain way; the pressure to pretend to be something you're not; the pressure to conform; the pressure to get good grades; the pressure to act cool at all costs. Pick out three types of pressure you think will be easiest to write about. (Remember you'll need to come up with specific details and examples to illustrate each.)

b. Write a thesis statement. Your thesis should be a clear statement of the three types of pressure you are going to write about. Here is an example:

> In my experience, many high-school students are made miserable by the pressure to be something they're not, the pressure to act cool, and the pressure to look a certain way.

c. List as many specific details and/or examples as you can think of for each type of pressure mentioned in your thesis. These lists will provide you with the supporting material for each paragraph.

d. Write a first draft of your essay. Remember to begin each supporting paragraph with a main-point statement. Here is an example of a first-draft essay:

> In my experience, many high-school students are made miserable by the pressure to be something they're not, the pressure to act cool, and the pressure to look a certain way.
>
> High school students are constantly pressured to be something that they are not. It doesn't matter who you are—there is pressure to change. If you're a good student, someone is pushing you to blow off classes and party more. If you party, somebody else is saying you you really ought to settle down and study. If you're a life-of-the-party type, they say you're just a clown. If you're a quiet reader type, somebody is telling you you ought to be more sociable. If you're going with somebody, people say "You shouldn't be so serious at this age. You should just date casually." If you date a lot of girls they say, "You're a player. You don't really care about anybody." If you drink or do drugs, people warn you that you're ruining your life. But if you don't use them, people say "What's the matter? Can't you handle it?" At an age when most students don't have a real strong self-image, the constant pressure to be somebody else is really hard to handle.
>
> High school students get a lot of pressure to act like they're cool. By cool I mean like they don't really care about anything. You can see it in the way the popular guys act. They stroll down the hall like they don't care if they ever get where they're going. If they see a friend, they don't actually say anything. They just raise their eyebrows a little. You're not supposed to show enthusiasm about anything. If you get a test back with an "A" on it, you're supposed to just grunt and put it into your notebook. If a teacher asks if you'd like to work on the school newspaper—even if you really would—you're supposed to shrug. People are afraid they'll be laughed at if they show excitement about anything.
>
> Girls talk a lot about how they are pressured to be thin and look like models. But guys get a lot of pressure to look a certain way, too. The same girls who complain about having to look like models hang around the muscular body-builder types. The guys who are tall and look older than their age are the most popular. So where does that leave guys who are skinny and on the short side? My brother had a real growth spurt the summer after he graduated from high school, and I'm just hoping that happens to me too. We also get a lot of pressure to wear the "right" clothes. It's ridiculous. Suddenly a $90 pair of basketball shoes is what you have to have. Or a windbreaker with a certain logo on it. Or a leather jacket. And then there's the "right" haircut. One week, a certain hair style is cool, and the next week it's just for losers. It's hard to keep your mind on your studies when you're trying to keep up with all the fashion trends.
>
> These are all kinds of pressures that high school students have to deal with.

e. If possible, lay your essay aside for a day or two. When you return to it, re-read it critically, asking yourself these questions:

— Does my thesis statement accurately indicate the main idea of my whole essay??
— Do each of my supporting paragraphs begin with its own topic sentence?
— Does every detail within a paragraph support that topic sentence? Or is there irrelevant material that needs to be *deleted?*
— Is the support of any of my paragraphs skimpy? Do I need to *add* more details?
— Do I need to correct errors in spelling, punctuation, or grammar?
— Is my language too slangy or informal?
— Have I used transitions between sentences and between paragraphs to tie my thoughts together?
— Have I written an effective introductory and concluding paragraph?

f. Revise your essay, correcting any weaknesses you've discovered. Here is a revision of the essay above. New material appears in **boldface** type.

> **Adults are always saying things like "The teenage years are the best years of your life." But** in my experience, **the teenage years are tough.** Many high-school students are made miserable by the pressure to be something they're not, the pressure to act cool, and the pressure to look a certain way.
>
> **First of all,** high school students are constantly pressured to be something that they are not. It doesn't matter who you are—there is pressure to change. If you're a good student, someone is pushing you to ~~blow off~~ **skip** classes and party more. If you party, somebody else is saying you you really ought to settle down and study. If you're a life-of-the-party type, they say you're just a clown. If you're a quiet reader type, somebody is telling you you ought to be more sociable. If you're going with somebody, people say "You shouldn't be so serious at this age. You should just date casually." If you date a lot of girls they say, "You're a player. You don't really care about anybody." If you drink or do drugs, people warn you that you're ruining your life. But if you don't use them, people say "What's the matter? Can't you handle it?" At an age when most students don't have a ~~real~~ **very** strong self-image, the constant pressure to be somebody else is really hard to handle.
>
> **Secondly,** high school students get a lot of pressure to act ~~like they're~~ cool. By cool I mean ~~like~~ as if they don't really care about anything. You can see it in the way the popular guys act. They stroll down the hall ~~like~~ as if they don't care if they ever get where they're going. If they see a friend, they don't actually say anything. They just raise their eyebrows a little. **To be cool,** you're not supposed to show enthusiasm about anything. If you get a test back with an "A" on it, you're supposed to just grunt and put it into your notebook. If a teacher asks if you'd like to work on the school newspaper—even if you really would—you're supposed to shrug. **It seems to me that this kind of cool is really fear.** People are afraid they'll be laughed at if they show excitement about anything.
>
> **A final kind of pressure in high school is the pressure to look a certain way.** Girls talk a lot about how they are pressured to be thin and look like models. But guys get a lot of pressure ~~to look a certain way,~~ too. The same girls who complain about having to look like models hang around the muscular body-builder types. The guys who are tall and look older than their age are the most popular. So where does that leave guys who are skinny and on the short side? ~~My brother had a real growth spurt the summer after he graduated from high school, and I'm just hoping that happens to me too.~~ We also get a lot of pressure to wear the "right" clothes. It's ridiculous. Suddenly a $90 pair of basketball shoes is what you have to have**,** ~~, Or~~ or a windbreaker with a certain logo on it**,** or ~~, Or~~ a leather jacket. And then there's the "right" haircut. One week, a certain hair style is cool, and the next week it's just for losers. It's hard to keep your mind on your studies when you're trying to keep up with all the fashion trends.
>
> These are all kinds of pressure that high school students have to deal with. **Combined, they make high school a difficult time and place for many teenagers.**

6   RESPONSIBILITY

Assignment

Write a paragraph about a time you have seen someone avoiding responsibility for his or her own problem. Begin with this topic sentence: "Just like M. Scott Peck, I have seen someone refuse to take responsibility for his (*or* her) own problem." Then go on to develop your paper by explaining who the person is, what the person's problem was, how he or she helped to create it, and how he or she blamed others or circumstances rather than accept responsibility.

Prewriting

Once you have a person or two in mind as possible subjects for this paragraph, ask yourself questions to generate the kind of detail you'll need. Here's one student's example of such self-questioning:

— <u>Whom</u> have I seen avoid responsibility? My cousin Allan.
— <u>When</u> did he avoid responsibility? Last summer.
— <u>What</u> was he avoiding responsibility for? Finding a summer job.
— <u>How</u> did he avoid responsibility? He didn't follow up on job leads; he showed up late or not at all for interviews; he "forgot" to put in applications; he slept all day instead of job-hunting; he was too picky about jobs
— <u>Who</u> or <u>what</u> did he blame? His parents, his car, the newspapers, the employers

After you have answered questions such as these, you will have plenty of material to draw on for your paragraph. (If you can't come up with answers, you may need to choose another subject.)

How to Proceed

a. You've already been provided with your topic sentence: *Just like M. Scott Peck, I have seen someone refuse to take responsibility for his (or her) own problem.* Now you need to come up with a second sentence that identifies the subject of your paragraph and briefly mentions the situation that he or she refused to take responsibility for, like this:

> When my cousin Allan was supposed to look for a job last summer, he blamed everyone but himself for his failure to find one.

b. In the rest of your paragraph, you will give specific details about your subject's irresponsible behavior. Be sure you mention not only how he or she evaded responsibility, but also how he or she tried to put the blame for the situation on someone or something else.

c. Wrap your paragraph up with a concluding statement. That statement might do one of several things. It could summarize what has come before. It could give a final thought of your own. Or it might predict what will happen in the future.

Here is a sample first draft based on this assignment:

> Just like M. Scott Peck, I have seen someone refuse to take responsibility for his own problem. When my cousin Allan was supposed to find a job last summer, he blamed everyone but himself for his failure to find one. He wouldn't look at the classified ads until the newspaper was several weeks old. Then when he would call about the job too late, he'd blame "the stupid newspaper." When someone else would tell him about a job opening, he'd screw that up too. When my uncle Joe told him the car wash was hiring, he said he wanted a desk job. When Joe blew up at him, Allan acted all hurt and said, "You want to see me stuck in a car wash my whole life?" Mrs. Whitaker actually lined up an interview for him at the

computer company where she works. He was more than a half hour late for it and told the interviewer, "I'm not much of a morning person." Needless to say, he didn't get the job, and guess who he blamed? Mrs. Whitaker. Although there were "Help Wanted" signs all over the neighborhood, he constantly "forgot" to put in applications anywhere. As the summer ended and it was clear that Allan wasn't going to get a job, my uncle Joe had an idea. He gave Allan the job of painting the house . . . for free.

d. Now re-read your paragraph, making sure it gives specific enough examples of your subject's evasion of responsibility. Be on the lookout, too, for mistakes in spelling and punctuation, slang or overly informal language, and a lack of helpful transitions. Here is a revised version of the above paragraph. New material appears in **boldface** type.

Just like M. Scott Peck, I have seen someone refuse to take responsibility for his own problem. When my cousin Allan was supposed to find a job last summer, he blamed everyone but himself for his failure to find one. He wouldn't look at the classified ads until the newspaper was several weeks old. Then when he would call too late about **a job that was advertised there**, he'd blame "the stupid newspaper." When someone else would tell him about a job opening, he'd ~~screw that up too~~ **find something wrong with it. For example,** when my uncle Joe told him the car wash was hiring, he said he wanted a desk job. When Joe ~~blew up~~ **got angry** at him, Allan acted all hurt and said, "You want to see me stuck in a car wash my whole life?" **Allan's neighbor,** Mrs. Whitaker, actually lined up an interview for him at the computer company where she works. He was more than a half hour late for it and told the interviewer, "I'm not much of a morning person." Needless to say, he didn't get the job, and guess who he blamed? Mrs. Whitaker. **And finally**, although there were "Help Wanted" signs all over the neighborhood, he constantly "forgot" to put in applications anywhere. **His excuse for that was that he was "too tired" or "too busy."** As the summer ended and it was clear that Allan wasn't going to get a job, my uncle Joe had an idea. He gave Allan the job of painting the house . . . for free.

7 ANXIETY: CHALLENGE BY ANOTHER NAME

Assignment

Write a paragraph in which you describe the process you went through when you were faced with a difficult decision. Be sure to discuss the following: what the decision was; why it was particularly difficult for you; the pros and cons of the options you considered; and, of course, the decision you finally made. Conclude by explaining how you feel now about the wisdom of your decision.

Prewriting

When you describe a process, as you will in this paragraph, you tell about a series of steps you went through. In order to get ready to write this paragraph, then, you need to identify what those particular steps were.

Once you have decided what difficult decision you will write about, make a list of the thoughts, events, or actions that were part of it. At this point, don't worry about the order the steps occurred in—just get them down on paper. One student decided to write about the time she needed to decide whether to break up with her boyfriend before he went off to college. Here is the list she created:

— Talked with Aunt Tina
— Overheard Tim
— Began thinking about breaking up
— Went out with Josh for two years
— Josh accepted at school two hundred miles away
— Saw what happened with Mike and Terri
— Worried about hurting Josh, being alone
— Talked with friends
— Talked with Mom
— Broke up with Josh

Next, go back and number the items in your list in the order in which they happened, like this:

9—Talked with Aunt Tina
4—Overheard Tim
5—Began thinking about breaking up
1—Went out with Josh for two years
3—Josh accepted at school two hundred miles away
2—Saw what happened with Mike and Terri
7—Worried about hurting Josh, being alone
6—Talked with friends
8—Talked with Mom
10—Broke up with Josh

Now that you have identified the order in which events involved in the decision were made, you are ready to begin writing.

How to Proceed

a. Decide on a topic sentence for your paragraph. In it, you should let your reader know what difficult decision you faced. Here's a sample:

> Last fall, I faced the hard decision of whether to break up with my boyfriend, Josh.

b. Write a rough draft of your paragraph. In it, you will need to do three things: (1) briefly explain the situation, (2) tell the steps you went through to make your decision, and (3) conclude by telling how you now feel about the decision you made. Your rough draft should look something like this:

> Last fall, I faced the decision of whether to break up with my boyfriend, Josh. It was a hard decision. But just as I was starting my senior year in high school, Josh was going to college in another state. At first I didn't think that would be any problem. I thought Josh would be home often, and I could go see him, and everything would be OK. But then I saw what happened to Mike and Terri. He and Terri swore they would never break up. But two months after he moved, Mike told Terri he was dating somebody else. Terri told me afterwards that a long-distance relationship could never work. I began wondering if Josh and I were nuts to try to continue going together. Then I went to a party our friends were having. While I was coming back from the bathroom, I overheard Tim talking to Mike. Tim was saying, "Mike, don't be an idiot. Melissa's a great girl, but you need to be a free man at college." I began thinking about myself, too. Was I going to go through my whole senior year without dating anyone? That didn't sound like much fun. So I began to think about breaking up with Josh. I talked with my mom and all my friends, but they weren't much help. They just said, "You have to do what's right for you." But finally I talked with my Aunt Tina, and her advice really reached me. She said, "You are 17, and Josh is 18. Your jobs in life right now are to grow and change, not to stay the same. When you're 25, you'll be a completely different person than you are now. Don't try to hang on to the present." The next day I told Josh I thought we should break up before he left for school. We both cried, but I think we were both relieved, too. Now he's off at college, and I do miss him. But Aunt Tina was right.

c. Re-read your paragraph, asking yourself the following questions:

— Have I adequately explained the decision I had to make?
— Have I made the reader understand why the decision was difficult?
— Have I explained the pros and cons of the different options I considered?
— Have I told what steps I went through in making my decision?
— Have I explained how I feel about my decision now?

d. Finally, read your paragraph aloud to yourself or a friend. Listen to it critically (or ask your friend to give his or her feedback.) Notice if you need to add transitions, such as "Later," "as a result," or "finally," to help your reader follow the sequence of events. Determine if you need to add or delete details. Double-check your spelling and punctuation, and consider adding a stronger opening point or concluding statement, and then write your final draft. Here is our student-writer's final draft. New material is shown in **boldface** type.

> Last fall, I faced the hard decision of whether to break up with my boyfriend, Josh. It was a ~~hard~~ **difficult** decision **because we had been together for two years, and I really cared for him**. But just as I was starting my senior year in high school, Josh was going to college in another state. At first I didn't think that would be any problem. I thought Josh would be home often, and I could go see him, and everything would be OK. But then I saw what happened to **my friends** Mike and Terri. **When Mike moved with his family to another city,** he and Terri swore they would never break up. But two months after he moved, Mike told Terri he was dating somebody else. Terri told me afterwards that a long-distance relationship could never work. I began wondering if Josh and I were ~~nuts~~ **foolish** to try to continue going together.

Then I went to a party our friends were having. While I was coming back from the bathroom, I overheard Tim talking to Mike. Tim was saying, "Mike, don't be an idiot. Melissa's a great girl, but you need to be a free man at college." **I wondered if Tim was right.** I began thinking about myself, too. Was I going to go through my whole senior year without dating anyone? That didn't sound like much fun. So I began to think about breaking up with Josh. I talked with my mom and all my friends, but they weren't much help. They just said, "You have to do what's right for you." But finally I talked with my Aunt Tina, and her advice really reached me. She said, "You are 17, and Josh is 18. Your jobs in life right now are to grow and change, not to stay the same. When you're 25, you'll be a completely different person than you are now. Don't try to hang on to the present." The next day I told Josh I thought we should break up before he left for school. We both cried, but I think we were both relieved, too. Now he's off at college, and I do miss him. But Aunt Tina was right. **My job right now is to grow and change, and I can't do that trying to hold on to somebody who is two hundred miles away.**

8   ALL THE GOOD THINGS

Assignment

Do you have any souvenir that, like Sister Helen's lists, you have kept for years? Write a paragraph about that souvenir. Start your paragraph with a topic sentence such as "_____ is one of my oldest and proudest possessions." Then describe just what the item is, how you originally obtained it, and where you keep it now. Most importantly, explain why the souvenir is precious to you.

Prewriting

Generate details about your souvenir by asking yourself a series of *who, what, when, where, why,* and *how* questions to which you write the answers. Make the questions appropriate to your subject. One student proceeded like this:

— <u>What is my souvenir?</u> A photograph.
— <u>Who is in the photograph?</u> Five girlfriends and me who all shared the middle name of "Ann."
— <u>When was the photograph taken?</u> When I was in fifth grade.
— <u>Why was the photograph taken?</u> We thought it was funny that so many of us had the same middle name, so we decided to get together for an "Ann" party. The six of us met at my house and my mom fixed us a special lunch. For dessert we had a cake with "Ann Rules!" written on it in frosting. My dad took the picture of us all sitting there laughing together.
— <u>Why have I kept this souvenir for so long?</u> Since the photograph was taken, all but one of the girls have moved away or are going to another school. The photograph is a way of remembering my friends from fifth grade.
— <u>Where do I keep the photograph?</u> In my photo album.

How to Proceed

a. Write a topic sentence for your paragraph that very briefly describes the souvenir you are going to write about, like this:

A souvenir that I have kept for many years is a photograph of six girls, all 11 or 12 years old.

b. Continue your paragraph by describing your souvenir in detail.

c. Conclude your paragraph by explaining why it is of value to you—in other words, why you have bothered to hang on to it. The girl writing about the photograph came up with this first draft:

A souvenir that I have kept for many years is a photograph of six girls, all 11 or 12 years old. They are sitting on a green sofa and each of them is laughing. The girls do not look much alike. What they do have in common is something you can't see in the photograph. Each of the girls has the middle name of Ann. They are Jacqueline Ann, Sue Ann, Lee Ann, Jo Ann and Joanne (we cheated a little to let her in), and me, Sarah Ann. We were all students in Mrs. Bennett's fifth-grade class. One day in class we took a poll to find out the most common names. That's when we discovered we had six Anns. We thought that was very funny, so we formed an Ann Club. The Ann Club didn't do very much except meet on the day that the photograph was taken. All the girls came to my house on a Saturday. My mom fixed us lunch. For dessert we had a cake that said "Ann Rules!" My dad took the picture of us after lunch. Except for Lee Ann I don't know where any of the other Anns are today. All of them either moved away or transferred to other schools. I keep the photo in my album and pull it out once in a while to look at it.

d. Reread your paragraph, asking yourself these questions:

— Have I described my souvenir, using rich detail so that a reader can easily picture it?
— Have I told where the souvenir came from, what circumstances surrounded it, and any people or places that were connected with it?
— Have I made my reader understand why the souvenir is special to me?
— Have I ended my paragraph with a suitable concluding thought?

e. Rewrite the paragraph as needed. Here is our student-author's revised work:

A souvenir that I have kept for many years is a photograph of six girls, all 11 or 12 years old. They are sitting on a **lumpy old** green sofa and ~~each of them is~~ **all of them are** laughing. The girls do not look much alike. **One is plump, one is very skinny, and four are sort of average. Two are black, one is Asian, and three are white.** What they do have in common is something you can't see in the photograph. Each of the girls has the middle name of Ann. They are Jacqueline Ann, Sue Ann, Lee Ann, Jo Ann and Joanne (we cheated a little to let her in), and me, Sarah Ann. We were all students in Mrs. Bennett's fifth-grade class. One day in class we took a poll to find out the most common names. That's when we discovered we had six Anns. We thought that was very funny, so we formed an Ann Club. The Ann Club didn't do very much except meet on the day that the photograph was taken. All the girls came to my house on a Saturday. My mom fixed us lunch. For dessert we had a cake that **had written on it in icing,** ~~said~~ "Ann Rules!" My dad took the picture of us after lunch. Except for Lee Ann**, who still goes to my high school,** I don't know where any of the other Anns are today. All of them either moved away or transferred to other schools. I keep the photo in my album and pull it out once in a while to look at it. **It always makes me smile to remember my fifth-grade friends named Ann.**

9   THE YELLOW RIBBON

Assignment

Vingo had to wait in suspense to discover something important about his future. When have you had the experience of waiting a long time (or what seemed like a long time) to find out something important? Such situations might have involved a grade for a project or a class, an award for which you were in the running, a part in a play, a question concerning your (or a loved one's) health, or an acceptance or rejection by a college or another important program. Write an essay about the situation. Tell the story a little at a time, as Hamill does, in order to keep the reader in suspense until the end. Begin by explaining what you were waiting for and why it was important. Continue by describing the wait and the emotions you experienced as time went by. Finish by telling how the wait finally ended and how you felt once it was over.

Prewriting

In order to remember the thoughts and feelings you experienced during this suspenseful time, spend some time freewriting. Without worrying about organization, spelling, punctuation, or the like, spend at least ten minutes simply writing anything that comes into your mind about the time you spent waiting for something important. Here is the freewriting done by one student about the time spent waiting for her mother's medical test results to come back:

> Boy was that a scary time. After it was over I think I didn't want to remember it any more so I haven't thought about it for a long time. First thing — walking in on Mom and Dad when they looked so upset. Mom had like a dozen doctor's appointments she kept saying it was just "ordinary female" stuff. Nobody told us kids anything but we knew something was wrong. Saw her crying once. She and Dad kept having these closed-door talks. Who finally found out what was going on? Jeremy? Big scene at the dinner table. Jessica freaked out. Then the wait for the biopsy results that went on forever. Screw-up at the lab. Everybody acting so weird. Dad trying to act normal HA. Jeremy yelled at Jessica. Everything that we did I'd think "is this the last time?" When we found out it was OK things still were weird. Everybody was like so on edge.

How to Proceed

a. Besides an introduction and a conclusion, your essay will include three main paragraphs. You'll need, then, to divide your story into three parts. One way to do that would be to use your first paragraph to explain what you were waiting for and why it mattered so much to you. Your second paragraph could describe the wait itself and your feelings during that time. The third paragraph could explain how the wait ended and how you felt about its conclusion.

b. Based on the division you've decided on, write a scratch outline for your essay, like this:

> <u>Thesis:</u> It was hard for my family to wait to find out if my mother had breast cancer.
>
> I.   Introduction
> II. Why we were waiting, and why it was important
> III. The wait itself
> IV. How the wait ended
> V.   Conclusion

c. Using your scratch outline as a guide, write a rough draft of your essay. Here is a sample:

>Last winter my family had to wait to find out if my mother had breast cancer.

>It took me a while to find out that anything was wrong with my mom. I didn't know it, but she had found a lump in her breast weeks before. Because some breast lumps are harmless, my parents didn't want to tell us kids anything until they knew for sure something was wrong. I knew my mom kept going off to doctor's appointments, she just kept saying it was for ordinary stuff. It became obvious that something bad was going on. I remember walking into the kitchen and finding my parents sitting at the table together, holding hands. One look at their faces told me something serious was going on. But suddenly I didn't want to know. I just pretended I didn't notice. I think it was that same day, though, that my brother Jeremy busted out at the dinner table. He said, "What is going on here? Is somebody dying or what?" Mom got all choked up, and Dad told us that Mom might have breast cancer. Mom's mother had died of breast cancer when she was only 50, so we knew how serious that was. I just sat there stunned, but my younger sister Jessica freaked out. She kept asking, "Are you going to die?" and Mom and Dad were trying to comfort her and Jeremy ended up yelling at Jessica about making everything worse.

>Once we knew what was going on, I think everyone felt better in a weird way. At least we felt like we were all in this together. It turned out that Mom had had a biopsy at the hospital. That's where they take a sample of the lump and test it to see if it's cancer or not. And now we were waiting for those results. They had told Mom that the results would be back in ten days. We marked the tenth day on the calendar with a big red circle. For what seemed like about a year we waited. Every time the phone rang, we jumped. Dad tried to act very normal and optimistic but he looked miserable. Jessica was practically hysterical every day. She'd laugh like crazy at the least little thing, and then burst out crying. Jeremy just looked glum. I felt lost and scared and lonely. Every time my mom and I would do anything together, like go to the grocery store, I'd think, "Is this the last time we'll do this?" Mom was actually the most together of us all. She seemed kind of peaceful, like she could accept whatever happened. Finally the ten days were over, but guess what? No results! There had been some sort of screw-up at the lab. That's when I really lost it. It was awful.

>Finally, on day twelve, I came home from school to find my mom sitting in the living room, crying. Immediately I started crying too. Then I felt my mom's arms around me. She said, "No, no! It's good news! I'm so sorry, honey—I was just crying from relief!" At first I didn't believe her, but as it sunk in I cried harder than ever. All the tension of the last two weeks just washed over me. We sat on the floor crying and laughing and hugging each other for the longest time.

>The next couple of weeks were pretty strange. We didn't just bounce back to normal right away. It was a pretty weird time.

d. Ask a friend to read your essay and answer these questions:

— Do I state my thesis in the opening paragraph?
— Does everything in my essay help to support that thesis?
— Do I provide good, clear details to help the reader understand why this period of waiting was difficult?
— Do I use transitional words and phrases (such as "Later," "At the same time," "But," "Another thing" and "Finally") to tie together my thoughts?
— Do I need a stronger introduction or conclusion?

e. Revise your essay until you are satisfied you have done your best work. Here is a revised version of the rough draft you've just read. New material appears in **boldface** type.

> **One of the most difficult experiences I've had occurred last winter, when** ~~Last winter~~ my family had to wait to find out if my mother had breast cancer.
>
> It took me a while to find out that anything was wrong with my mom. I didn't know it, but she had found a lump in her breast weeks before. Because some breast lumps are harmless, my parents didn't want to tell us kids anything until they knew for sure something was wrong. I knew my mom kept going off to doctor's appointments, **but** she just kept saying it was for ordinary stuff. It became obvious that something bad was going on. I remember walking into the kitchen and finding my parents sitting at the table together, holding hands. One look at their faces told me something serious was going on. But suddenly I didn't want to know. I just pretended I didn't notice. I think it was that same day, though, that my brother Jeremy ~~busted~~ **burst** out at the dinner table. He said, "What is going on here? Is somebody dying or what?" Mom got all choked up, and Dad told us that Mom might have breast cancer. Mom's mother had died of breast cancer when she was only 50, so we knew how serious that was. I just sat there stunned, but my younger sister Jessica freaked out. **She cried and screamed and** ~~She~~ kept asking, "Are you going to die?" ~~and~~ Mom and Dad were trying to comfort her and Jeremy ended up yelling at Jessica about making everything worse.
>
> Once we knew what was going on, I think everyone felt better in a weird way. At least we felt ~~like~~ **as if** we were all in this together. It turned out that Mom had had a biopsy at the hospital. That's where they take a sample of the lump and test it to see if it's cancer or not. And now we were waiting for those results. ~~They~~ **The people at the hospital** had told Mom that the results would be back in ten days. We marked the tenth day on the calendar with a big red circle. For what seemed like about a year**,** we waited. Every time the phone rang, we jumped. Dad tried to act very normal and optimistic**,** but he looked miserable. Jessica was practically hysterical every day. She'd laugh like crazy at the least little thing, and then burst out crying. Jeremy just looked glum. I felt lost and scared and lonely. Every time my mom and I would do anything together, like go to the grocery store, I'd think, "Is this the last time we'll do this?" Mom was actually the ~~most together~~ **calmest** of us all. She seemed kind of peaceful, ~~like~~ **as if** she could accept whatever happened. Finally the ten days were over, but guess what? No results! There had been some sort of ~~screw-up~~ **problem** at the lab. That's when I really lost ~~it~~ **control.** ~~It was awful.~~ **I couldn't eat or sleep for two days.**
>
> Finally, on day twelve, I came home from school to find my mom sitting in the living room, crying. Immediately I started crying ~~too~~ **so hard I couldn't even see. I just dropped all my school books and collapsed on the floor.** Then I felt my mom's arms around me. She said, "No, no! It's good news! I'm so sorry, honey—I was just crying from relief!" At first I didn't believe her, but as it sunk in I cried harder than ever. All the tension of the last two weeks just washed over me. We sat on the floor crying and laughing and hugging each other for the longest time.
>
> The next couple of weeks were pretty strange. We didn't just bounce back to normal right away. ~~It was a pretty weird time.~~ **Everyone walked and talked very quietly. It was as if we'd all been sick and needed time to rest and get better. I haven't thought about this period in my life for a long time now. It was a time I felt how fragile life is, and that was a scary realization.**

10   AN ELECTRONIC FOG HAS SETTLED OVER AMERICA

Assignment

Maguire made an effort to get his family to reduce its TV watching and to read more, but the essay suggests that his attempt came too late. If you have children some day (or if you already have them), what are several qualities or habits that you strongly hope that they will possess? How will you try to instill these qualities or habits in your children? Write an essay that explains both what these hoped-for characteristics are, and, as specifically as possible, how you will encourage your children to develop these characteristics.

Prewriting

Begin developing your ideas for this assignment by spending a few minutes making two lists: one of *qualities* and one of *habits* that you think are valuable for a person of any age to have. Here are some examples:

Qualities

Honesty
Compassion
Sense of humor
Ambition
Common sense

Habits

Being physically active
Reading
Playing sports
Keeping up with news
Going to church
Eating a good diet
Traveling

How to Proceed

a. Now, review your lists and ask yourself, "What three items from these lists would I most like my children to have?" Once you have chosen your three items, write a thesis statement for your essay, like this:

When I have children, it will be important to me to that they read regularly, be involved in sports, and do some volunteer work.

b. Your essay will be made up of five paragraphs, with paragraphs 2–4 each addressing one of the three qualities or habits you have chosen. Write a scratch outline for your essay. The outline for the essay based on the above thesis statement would look like this:

Thesis: When I have children, it will be important to me to that they read regularly, be involved in sports, and do some volunteer work.

   I. Introduction
   II. Regular reading
   III. Involvement in sports
   IV. Volunteer work
   V. Conclusion

c. As you write the first draft of your essay, you will provide details about why you think each of the qualities or habits you have chosen is important, and specifically how you will encourage your children to develop them. Here is the first draft of the essay outlined above:

> If I ever have children, it will be important to me that they read regularly, be involved in sports, and do some volunteer work.
>
> First, reading regularly. The advantages of being a good reader are too many to count. Children who read well naturally do better in all of their classes. They can simply understand the textbooks better than poor readers. I've also heard that reading well actually helps people develop good thinking skills, because readers constantly have to work mentally to turn those little black marks on the page into words. I plan to encourage my children to read in several ways. First, I will begin reading to them as soon as they are born. Even just showing picture books to a baby and talking to him about it. Secondly, I will be sure that my children see me read. Third, I will make sure that there is good reading material in the house. I'll have a library of interesting books, and I'll subscribe to magazines they might be interested in. And finally, I will limit the time they are allowed to watch TV. I think kids who watch too much TV never take the time to develop their reading skills.
>
> Secondly, I want my children to be involved in at least one sport. I think playing sports is valuable in a number of ways. It keeps children active, and that's good for them. Learning to be at least halfway decent at a sport makes a kid feel like he's accomplished something. And being part of a team helps teach children about cooperating with others and being a good sport. I will work with them at home to make sure they know a little bit about the basic skills involved in a sport before they go out for a team. Also, I'll be aware of community teams, like soccer or baseball teams, that they can be involved in during the summer. And finally, I'll take them along to watch when my buddies and I play basketball or softball.
>
> I have been lucky enough to grow up in a family where we had plenty to eat, nice clothes to wear, and a comfortable house to live in. I hope I'll be able to give those things to my kids, too. But it bothers me to see kids who have grown up "comfortably" take their good luck for granted. I've got some nieces and nephews like that, and it drives me crazy. They whine all the time about wanting more stuff, instead of being grateful. I don't want my kids to be like that. I want them to realize that if they're lucky enough to have more than they need in life, they ought to share with people who have less. To encourage them to do that, I will take them along when they are little when I do volunteer work. When they're old enough to do some volunteer activities of their own, I think I might make it a house rule that they should. Maybe I'll tie it into their earning an allowance or something.
>
> All in all, I think that if my kids become regular readers, play sports, and learn to do some volunteering, they will be better off.

d. Put your essay aside for a day or two and then re-read it, asking yourself these questions:

— Does my thesis statement clearly state the main idea of my essay?
— Do paragraphs 2–4 all begin with their own topic sentences?
— Does every detail in paragraphs 2–4 help support that topic sentence?
— Have I explained in each paragraph not only why a quality or habit is important to me, but how I plan to encourage it in my children?
— Have I used transitional words or phrases to tie my thoughts together?
— Do I need to include a stronger introduction and conclusion?
— Is my essay free of errors in spelling, grammar, and punctuation?

e. Revise your essay until you are satisfied that you have done your best work. Here is our student-author's revised essay. New material appears in **boldface**.

Every father has different priorities for his children. Those priorities reveal some of the things that are most important in our own lives. In my case, if I ever have children, it will be important to me that they read regularly, be involved in sports, and do some volunteer work.

First, **I want my children to read** ~~reading~~ regularly. The advantages of being a good reader are too many to count. Children who read well naturally do better in all of their classes. They can simply understand the textbooks better than poor readers. **They are also better prepared for school, just because they have a better background of knowledge from their own reading.** I've also heard that reading well actually helps people develop good thinking skills, because readers constantly have to work mentally to turn those little black marks on the page into words. I plan to encourage my children to read in several ways. First, I will begin reading to them as soon as they are born. Even just showing picture books to a baby and talking to him about ~~it~~ **the books will help give him the idea that reading is worthwhile and fun.** Secondly, I will be sure that my children see me read. **Instead of turning on the TV after dinner, I'll sit down with a book or a newspaper.** Third, I will make sure that there is good reading material in the house. I'll have a library of interesting books, **like adventure stories and biographies,** and I'll subscribe to magazines **like <u>Sports Illustrated</u> and <u>People</u>** that ~~they~~ **my kids** might be interested in. And finally, I will limit the time they are allowed to watch TV. I think kids who watch too much TV never take the time to develop their reading skills.

Secondly, I want my children to be involved in at least one sport. I think playing sports is valuable in a number of ways. It keeps children active and ~~that's good for them~~. **helps them become physically fit.** Learning to be at least ~~halfway decent~~ **competent** at a sport makes a kid feel like he's accomplished something. And being part of a team helps teach children about cooperating with others and being a good sport. **In order to encourage them to get involved in sports,** I will work with them at home to make sure they know a little bit about the basic skills involved in a sport before they go out for a team. Also, I'll be aware of community teams, like soccer or baseball teams, that they can be involved in during the summer. And finally, I'll take them along to watch when my buddies and I play basketball or softball. **I hope if they see me enjoying it, they will be inclined to try it themselves.**

Finally, I want my kids to get into the habit of volunteering in the community. I have been lucky enough to grow up in a family where we had plenty to eat, nice clothes to wear, and a comfortable house to live in. I hope I'll be able to give those things to my kids, too. But it bothers me to see kids who have grown up "comfortably" take their good luck for granted. ~~I've got some nieces and nephews like that, and it drives me crazy. They whine all the time about wanting more stuff, instead of being grateful.~~ I don't want my kids to be like that. I want them to realize that if they're lucky enough to have more than they need in life, they ought to share with people who have less. To encourage them to do that, I will take them along when they are little when I do volunteer work. **For example, if I'm helping to serve a meal at a soup kitchen, they can come along and do little things like set the table. Then we'll talk about why I go there, and why I think they should, too.** When they're old enough to do some volunteer activities of their own, I think I might make it a house rule that they should. Maybe I'll tie it into their earning an allowance ~~or something~~.

All in all, **I want my children to be well-informed, active, healthy, and compassionate people.** I think ~~that if my kids become regular readers, play sports, and learn to do some volunteering, they will be better off~~. **that the habits of regular reading, playing sports, and volunteering in their communities will help them develop in those directions.**

Notes